Love to Hate the Boss

Strategies for Direct Reports.
Strategies for Bosses.

Strategies to Harmonize Your Workplace.

Dennis E. Gilbert

Published in the United States of America.

North Charleston, South Carolina, USA

ISBN: 1481188844
ISBN-13: 978-1481188845
LCCN: 2013900663

For everyone seeking a new perspective.

~Dennis E. Gilbert

CONTENTS

Preface   vii

Acknowledgments   ix

1   The Concept of Loving to Hate   1

2   Is Anyone Listening?   11

3   Decisions and Debates   27

4   Diplomatic Delegation   43

5   Bestowing Empowerment   59

6   Dress for Success   87

7   Overlooked for Advancement   103

8   You're Not My Boss   131

9   Some in the Family   145

10   Being a Sirius Performer   157

Notes   171

Index   179

About the Author   185

PREFACE

This book is not about hatred. It is not about love.

This is a business book. It is about getting the most from your job, your career, and your workplace. It is about making changes, dreaming big, and accomplishing more.

This book is about strategies. Strategies to help you cope, adapt, or break free. It is a book about workplace survival and harmony; it is about achieving organizational excellence.

I wrote it for direct reports. I wrote it for bosses. I wrote it for *you*.

Dennis E. Gilbert

ACKNOWLEDGMENTS

Life is a journey. The people I have met along the way have certainly shaped who I am today. I am thankful to have known people who have inspired me and encouraged me to reach for more.

I am forever grateful for my friends and family. I have learned and grown so much because of your contributions along the way. I believe that our journey shapes us, or at least it has shaped me.

Thank you to all of the people in workplaces everywhere who have shared a story of their journey with me. Thank you to those people who have stayed after a workshop or talked with me during a break. Thank you to the people I have sat beside on an airplane or chatted with in an elevator. Thank you to those who have telephoned me or e-mailed me when you've been excited about a new opportunity or sad because something didn't work out.

All of you have taught me about laughter, happiness, sadness, confidence, kindness, fear, success, taking chances, and risk.

Thank you to everyone who has been a part of my life and my journey. You have brought life to my thoughts and experiences; because of you this book was possible.

CHAPTER 1

THE CONCEPT OF LOVING TO HATE

"It is better to be hated for what you are than to be loved for what you are not."

~André Gide, *Autumn Leaves*[1]

Loving to hate is nothing new. People seem to be fascinated, obsessed, or culturally driven to create a pack, a following, or a group that invests in hating someone or something that they find distasteful or unwanted. In some cases, this may be the complete opposite of a once-loving obsession. This may develop from burnout, a new (unexpected) discovery, or a closer examination and consideration of what someone or something truly represents. In still other cases, people may love, hate, and return to loving that very same person, place, or thing.

Sometimes it seems to be about making a point. A point that people should follow someone else's lead, join the group, or get lost. Making a point often costs people and organizations in spiritual and tangible resources such as human energy, emotions, and time.

PEOPLE CHALLENGES IN THE WORKPLACE

This book is not about hatred. It is not about love. This book is not about bullying or mobbing, terrorism or peace. This book is about helping people learn to cope in their workplaces and to discover ways that they can improve their contribution, ways that they can create their success. It is about helping direct reports improve; it is about helping bosses improve. There may be many things in the workplace that you simply love to hate. These may represent your pet peeves or things other people do that drive you crazy.

People often run from challenges, misunderstandings, or conflicts, but when you are in pursuit of success you need to face your challenges and discover ways to overcome them. Doing anything else is simply unproductive.

CREATING YOUR SUCCESS

Everyone defines success in their own unique ways. The choices we make and the level of success we obtain may have more to do with our acceptance of responsibility than with luck.

We have a responsibility to pay our bills, obey laws, and, for most of us, earn a living. If we obtain a certain level of success, we typically assume additional responsibilities. This sounds like a no-brainer, but many do not recognize the depth of responsibility that comes with achievement. Subconscious avoidance of responsibility may derail performance, limiting future opportunities to achieve success.

Here are a few examples:

1. We want the managerial position, but we know with that job there is an expectation of extra hours and more community involvement.

2. We want the house with the big yard, but we then have a responsibility for the care and maintenance, which takes away from our leisure time or adds expense to our household budget.

3. We want the shiny new sports car, but with it we know comes extra washing, waxing,

and maintenance to keep it looking and performing its best.

Success does not come easily, and when we achieve it (depending, of course, on how we define it) it typically comes with additional responsibility. Not only does our fear of choices and fear of success affect the decisions we make, but so does the responsibility to perform. Remember, everyone defines success differently, but those who want true success know that it costs.

REMEMBER, EVERYONE DEFINES SUCCESS DIFFERENTLY, BUT THOSE WHO WANT TRUE SUCCESS KNOW THAT IT COSTS.

LOVING TO HATE

Successful employees, whether they are the boss, a direct report, or in the middle, being both a boss and a direct report, need to be aware of the dangers of loving to hate. Defining a love to hate ideology has its challenges. There are so many elements of the concept, most of which may seem apparent, but with so many possible definitions exploring a few will help set the tone for the concept.

SPORTS TEAMS

Basketball, football, and baseball teams all may fall victim to the love-to-hate ideology. People develop a passionate hate for opposing teams, teams that have winning records, teams that have losing records, and teams that they once loved but now hate. Players change, owners change, and some even come and go. Some teams develop a following and some don't; some develop a base of loving fans and some develop hating rivals.

POLITICAL FIGURES

Since at the time of this writing we are just spinning off the 2012 presidential election, the surge in loving to hate political figures is almost overwhelming. People love a candidate, and then they hate a candidate; they ask others for opinions and they give opinions even when they are not asked for. Some love with reasons; some don't really care. Some will love regardless of the facts and some will love to hate.

BRANDS

The motorcycle manufacturer Harley-Davidson has created a love-to-hate brand. Arthur Davidson and his friend William Harley began working on motor-driven bicycles around 1901.[2] The Harley-Davidson brand has seen many changes during more than a century in business. Once ridiculed by fans of Japanese motorcycles for "marking their spot" with leaked oil when parked, Harley-Davidson motorcycles are now an American icon.

Not only are these motorcycles highly sought after and in some cases highly priced, but the company has created a legacy of marketing and brand building with clothing, riding apparel, and parts and accessories, some of which make the bikes look good and some of which improve performance. They have established a cult like following and groups of enthusiasts are passionate about the brand.

FASHION

If fashion is your passion, you will no doubt be predisposed to the concept of loving to hate. Fashion changes from season to season, year to year, and it may also be somewhat driven by socioeconomic factors and demographics. Many people believe that fashion is cyclical. What was once beloved and popular grows old, stale, and hated.

Let's not leave out the cost and stigma associated with both high- and low-priced garments. People form images of fashion, represented by models, stereotypes of glamour or style, and the lifestyles associated with those who wear them. Some crave the latest style while others avoid being trendy and stick with what is simple and perhaps unnoticed. Some love items that look used and some love items that look brand new.

In fashion it would seem that for every love there is a hate. There are brands, and there are designers; there are leathers with fabric liners; there are overcoats made from goats, and plastic shoes that make world news. What one person loves, the other person hates; wear it enough and your love may turn to hate.

RULES

Rules should be simple, or so it would seem. For every rule that someone loves, someone else may love to hate it.

Several years ago some of the residents in my township started a ban on what is known in suburban America as "burner barrels." This classic yard trash décor typically consists of an old oil barrel with the top cut out. The idea is, or was in my neighborhood, to dispose of your paper trash by burning it in the burner barrel.

While unpopular in some circles, this practice was fully embraced in others. Personally, I love to hate whoever pursued this ban and took away my right to burn. All I see are dollar signs as I pay money to dispose of things that I do not want, especially junk mail. When I used to burn my trash there was a feeling of retaliation or vengeance against those unwanted items and perhaps even against the people who sent them. Make no mistake: people love to hate the rules.

BOOKS

The most talked about bestseller of the summer of 2012 was a book titled *Fifty Shades of Grey*, by the British author E.L. James.[3] While the summer beach resorts, airplanes, airports, backpacks, women's lingerie drawers, and man purses busted at the seams with copies of this novel, others loved to hate it.

It makes you wonder, what is the psychology behind loving to hate? Is there a method to this madness or does it stem from people's fear, envy, or greed about something that they don't understand or are otherwise unable to accept? Books can spark an interesting love-to-hate discussion.

MUSCIANS AND MOVIE STARS

Who could hate Bob Marley, Eminem, Justin Timberlake, or Kid Rock? Who could hate Faith Hill, Taylor Swift, or Celine Dion? Surprisingly, or maybe not, there are many people who love to hate these musical stars.

Movie stars may also become victims of the love-to-hate rage. Some of this could be because of roles that they play, characters they represent, or off-screen behavior that doesn't align with others' values or beliefs. We see people go crazy over Johnny Depp, Taylor Lautner, and Angelina Jolie. Reasons may abound, but regardless the concept of love to hate is ever present with our movie star icons.

THE CONCEPT

People love to hate many things. They love to hate sports teams, political figures, brands, fashion, rules, books, musicians, and movie stars. They hate the details, commitments, responsibilities, and outcomes of their own lives. They sometimes hate things they once cherished or loved and sometimes they hate for reasons no one seems to understand. People hate many things, and some people get pleasure from the hatred, they love to hate.

THEY SOMETIMES HATE THINGS THEY ONCE CHERISHED OR LOVED AND SOMETIMES THEY HATE FOR REASONS NO ONE SEEMS TO UNDERSTAND.

I have purposely left out many aspects of loving to hate, aspects such as race, religion, ethnicity, and age. Many of us have seen personal values grow, shrink, and change. Economic climates, societal and generational differences all may be contributing factors as we examine our values. Many have witnessed discrimination on the basis of race, age, and gender. These are societal issues that are important, but they are not destined for inclusion in this book.

This book is not about creating a position, movement, or ideology of hate. In fact, it is quite the contrary. It is about creating awareness and understanding that sometimes our passion of love, or of hate, of anything that goes against the flow, against the norm, or against societal standards may be more than just a paradox. It may be what moves, drives, inspires, and motivates us.

Loving to hate the boss may result in more productivity, less productivity, demotions, and promotions. People in workplaces everywhere are struggling. They struggle to survive, when what they really desire is to thrive. Many feel pressured, stressed, burnt-out, frustrated, and disengaged. After days, weeks, months, and sometimes years, they have found it pleasurable to hate. However, hate will not help them achieve success or maintain sanity.

You see, this book and the awareness that it creates will help you explore options, discover fixes, and exceed expectations. Love them or hate them, if you are one, or never will be one, there is value to understanding more about what makes people love to hate the boss.

CHAPTER 2

IS ANYONE LISTENING?

"When people talk, listen completely. Most people never listen."

~Ernest Hemingway[1]

Listening is a developed skill; it is not the same thing as hearing. Considering that we do not have a handicap or disability, hearing is instinctual. We hear sound, we hear noises. Listening requires us to concentrate. It requires us to try to understand what the other person is thinking, feeling, or attempting to express. If you have ever listened to a friend or family member with a problem and you've tried to help, you know this can be hard work; you may feel exhausted after listening.

In our personal lives and in the workplace, people often do not listen with the intent to understand. They may filter out many of the words, only keying in on items that are directly related to their needs or interests. They may hear things that are not said. They may hear the words they most hope for or most fear. One of the biggest problems and complaints is that people simply do not listen. People often listen to develop their response or rebuttal; but they may not be listening to understand.

Many workplace factors can affect our capacity to listen. A few that come to mind are power, timing, and reciprocity. Power may be an issue that affects listening. Sometimes we may have the right idea, but the timing is wrong. Reciprocity can be important, and so can the simple concept of whether or not it's a good idea.

POWER—BEING HEARD

"Nearly all men can stand adversity, but if you want to test a man's character, give him power."

~Abraham Lincoln[2]

Power is perhaps one of the most interesting factors in workplace success. There are two sides of power: a positive influence and a negative influence.

On the positive side, we may experience the overwhelming feeling of inspiration when we see or feel power. This may occur when we meet successful people or when the business owner or CEO comes to the workplace for a visit. The negative side may find us being turned off by a pushy co-worker or a bullying boss.

Power in our job roles may be formal or informal. Formal power typically relates to positional power. You are designated as a supervisor, manager, or other higher level of authority. Informal power may develop when someone is not designated as a boss, but they may have knowledge, skills, or tenure that positions them above others. It is important to remember that we all possess some form of power; and appropriately using it, formal or informal, will increase the likelihood of being heard.

Nearly every employee of any business or organization, of any job role or position, has at one time felt their suggestions or ideas go unnoticed. This feeling of being discounted, discarded, and even disrespected is not uncommon. One method to overcome this feeling and make a difference in our job role is to exert some form of power.

The obvious form of power is positional or formal. We are the boss—we say what, we say when, and we say how. This is also sometimes referred to as authoritarian leadership, a method of leadership that today is often considered outdated and is not well received. Popular wisdom also suggests that an authoritarian approach can cause disharmony between people of different generations when working together.

What this all means is that positional power is valuable but if misused, overused, or abused, it is a path for cultural disaster. If you have positional power, you can certainly flex your muscle to ensure your ideas are heard. In the absence of positional power, you still have opportunities to make your case, but you may have to rely on sources of informal power, persuasion, and influence.

Often we feel discouraged about presenting ideas when we lack formal power, but our success today depends more and more on our ability to get things done. This is also true as it relates to presenting or selling our ideas.

RIGHT IDEA—WRONG TIMING!

We have probably all heard or said the old cliché "timing is everything." In January 2011, the movie *Country Strong* and its associated soundtrack brought forward the lyrics of a Garret Hedlund song: "Timing is Everything."[3] If you have watched the movie or heard the song you may have discovered a new or different appreciation for timing.

Timing can have a profound effect on the outcome of situations we encounter both personally and professionally. The forces that apply pressure to people and organizations can quickly alter their needs or desires, which ultimately may allow acceptance or rejection of ideas. Within organizations, we see the forces of change altering paths and directions through leadership, vision, and performance outcomes. Externally, people and organizations may feel the force of change through technology, government regulations, and changing economic conditions.

Timing changes everything. Once upon a time we smoked on airplanes, purchased 5¼" floppy discs, and used pay phones while traveling. Today none of those represents a novel idea. Ideas and activities associated with the wrong timing are quickly put to rest. People and organizations will express their lack of interest or otherwise just ignore anything that is inappropriate for the time.

PEOPLE AND ORGANIZATIONS WILL EXPRESS THEIR LACK OF INTEREST OR OTHERWISE JUST IGNORE ANYTHING THAT IS INAPPROPRIATE FOR THE TIME.

Many ideas simply go unrepresented, not discussed, and discarded. We have a thought, we sort through it in our mind, and sometimes with a feeling of discouragement or weakened self-confidence, we decide it is not worthy of being presented. Many factors may drive a decision to disengage and be reluctant to bring forward new ideas. Everything from the fear of separation from the group to a negative fantasy that we may be blacklisted or fired for mentioning something so far from reality. Sadly, some ideas are never brought to the table.

In still other cases, we are enthusiastic about our idea and we charge forward with childlike excitement and anticipation, confident that we have the next big thing. In some cases we do have the next big thing and the timing is perfect, but in other cases our timing is off.

Do you have an idea? Before your next dash to the boss's office or the painstaking development of a presentation to the board of directors, consider the timing. Appropriate timing and successfully selling your idea may be contingent on many factors. These factors could include current or forecasted economic conditions, the timing in a fiscal cycle, pending governmental regulations, and world events. Timing may not be everything, but it is critically important.

YOUR NETWORK

"I'm not friends with the big boss."

While it may not be in everyone's best interest to attempt to get a seat at the dinner table with the big boss, being connected and developing your network is an important step to being seen and heard. The concept of building your personal network has never been more popular.

People are continuing to build their networks through face-to-face communication and also through internet tools such as Facebook, LinkedIn, and Twitter. Building a social media presence has many pros and cons. On the pros side, it helps to open new relationships that may not otherwise become possible and makes it easy for you to keep others updated about what is happening in your world. What sometimes is a pro may also be a con, as many people do not want others to know what they are doing, where they are traveling, or even to see pictures of family and friends. I feel very sure that the debate will continue for some time.

Do you want to be connected? Should you be more connected? If you are serious about your career path, the answer to both of these should be yes. If you really don't care much about your career and are simply trying to survive in your current job, the answer is maybe. If you have attained great wealth and want to hide away never to be found again, the answer is probably no.

As of September 2012, Facebook reports that they have more than one billion user accounts.[4] If Facebook were a country, it would currently rank third in terms of population[5], just behind China and India. The United States of America would rank fourth. Underestimating the power and capabilities that a reach of this magnitude has could be detrimental, assuming of course that you want to be found. A question I often ask people who are interested in advancing their career but remain apprehensive about social media is this: "Can you afford not to be using social media?"

Let us not forget traditional face-to-face networking. One of the most powerful methods for building relationships, in-person meetings give us the opportunity to make a good first impression. Face-to-face time has not lost its luster or its effectiveness. In fact, many people are building both traditional and social media networks by leveraging each platform. Traditional methods lead to new connections online and online connections may sometimes result in face-to-face meetings.

The ultimate goal is to build your network in an attempt to gain recognition and, hopefully, acceptance of your ideas. Getting connected means building relationships, and it is important to remember that these relationships are both push and pull in nature. Be sure to demonstrate genuine interest in your relationships, not just using them to push your ideas, products, or services. Are you appropriately connected?

RECIPROCITY

"The rule says that we should try to repay, in kind, what another person has provided us."

~Robert B. Cialdini[6]

Sales professionals do it every day; they persuade someone to buy their ideas, goods, or services. Some people never recognize the power of influence, and others experience a feeling of envy when they realize they are not up to the challenge of selling. Every day we make decisions and choices; we decide about our clothing, our food, and sometimes our schedule for the day. Influencing decisions and choices is sometimes easy, sometimes hard, and often requires negotiation. Selling our ideas sometimes requires influencing or persuading our target audience.

SELLING OUR IDEAS SOMETIMES REQUIRES INFLUENCING OR PERSUADING OUR TARGET AUDIENCE.

In the year 2000, the American film *Pay It Forward*[1] launched into the hearts of many who watched the concept of networking through the gift of good deeds. It is the idea that rather than pay back a favor, you pay it forward to a third party. This concept is somewhat in contrast to reciprocity theory, but nonetheless may be viable for consideration when selling your ideas.

Persuasion is powerful, and many factors may be involved in persuading someone to like your idea. Consider the idea of reciprocity or paying it forward. I do a good deed for you; you owe me one. I do a good deed for someone else, and they may in turn do a good deed for a third party. If we build upon others' ideas and concepts, does it help to sell our own? Perhaps, and more importantly a little reciprocity, a little influence, and a little persuasion never hurts.

Effectively using our network, we stand a good chance of being able to create a harmonious environment that engages others in the process of promoting our ideas, all through the concept of goodwill. The magic is created when people genuinely want to promote our ideas, not because we asked, but because they believe in us. In some business or recreational circles we call this a sponsor. A person or entity that believes enough in our cause to support and promote it without being asked. Delivered to the proper channel, there is seemingly nothing more powerful, and that power comes through belief and feeling, without any cost, obligation, or direct benefit.

HAVING GOOD IDEAS

I was in my early twenties and visiting my sister. Standing on her porch, I jumped on a teenager's bicycle and began to demonstrate that I could ride it down several steps from her porch leading to the sidewalk below. When the front tire hit the sidewalk I was catapulted over the handlebars and landed with a rather uncomfortable feeling. A voice broken by intense laughter asked, "Why did you to that?" My response was, "I thought it was a good idea at the time."

Most people are very passionate about their ideas. After all, if they have thought of it, it must be a good idea. There is some risk in presenting too many ideas. If it is a corporate brainstorming or strategy session, perhaps the floor is wide open, but in a general sense the presentation of too many ideas can lead to a label or stereotype that you wouldn't enjoy. Like the boy who cried wolf, consistent presentation of ideas, suggestions, and advice that is unsolicited may lead to others tuning you out whenever they hear you say, "I have an idea!" Unstoppable business vision and ideas that just spill out all over the place from your cognitive juices may need to be regulated for appropriate volume. If you have difficulty in your ideas being heard or valued you may already be facing this type of challenge.

Ideas need to be good, and good ideas sell themselves. There is no need for a lot of strategy about how, when, or why; open up the gates and let it out. Our challenge becomes realistic assessment of our ideas, keeping in mind that our personal conviction for an idea is probably already present, and timing is important.

Some may argue that there are no bad ideas. After all, ideas can be accepted or rejected, but most importantly they need to be heard. Ideas that are heard come in just the right quantities and typically have characteristics such as being visionary, timely, easily understood, and precise. Bad ideas tend to have opposing characteristics such as being risky, confusing, or too complex.

LISTENING AND UNDERSTANDING YOU

The tension at the twelve-person conference table was intense. The vice president always started the meeting by allowing the management team and other key staff to briefly discuss recent department activity. As the team leaders each waited their turn to speak, Tom, a reasonably well-respected manager became angry as one of the other team leaders, Jane, politely mentioned some challenges her team faced while working with Tom's department. Tom, agitated and upset, sat up straight in his chair, leaned forward, and stared at Jane's mouth. He was not listening; instead he was waiting for Jane's lips to stop moving so that he could blast her with his rebuttal. People sometimes believe that listening is the same thing as hearing. Often we use these words interchangeably without paying attention to the difference. Hearing typically refers to the instinctive process of hearing noise or sound. Assuming we are without any handicaps or disability, hearing comes to us naturally. Listening is somewhat different and may be described as a skill that is developed. Being a good listener often takes practice and, more importantly, requires our focus and energy when done properly.

Honest and accurate self-assessment is a critical skill for anyone in the workplace. When asked to self-assess, are you honest with yourself about your skills and competencies? Is your assessment accurate? Do you recognize your strengths and weaknesses?

Make sure you understand *you*. If someone accuses you of not listening, frequently interrupting, or often misunderstanding their thoughts or feelings, you may not be an effective listener. Failure to recognize shortcomings in listening skills will limit your workplace success.

CHAPTER SUMMARY

You may feel like no one is listening. Many reasons may exist for this feeling, and in some cases that feeling may be the reality. Power, timing, your network, reciprocity, quality of ideas, and listening skills (yours and others') may have an impact on the outcomes of your ideas.

After unsuccessful attempts at sharing your ideas, you may become discouraged; you may develop distaste for the boss or others involved. There are lessons in listening for the boss and for the direct report. Here are some questions to ask yourself as you consider if anyone is listening.

▶ Regarding power when presenting your next big idea:

1) Am I providing a solution, not just a reiteration of the problem?

2) Does my idea align with the larger organizational strategies? Is there a direct link to my proposed idea and business results?

3) Consider the situation from the other person's point of view. What questions would you ask?

▶ The timing of your next big idea:

4) Is this an original idea, and how does it contribute to or complement the mission and vision of the organization?

5) Economically, is the timing right? Do the current economic conditions of the organization or external economic climate support this idea?

6) If it was your money, or your investment in this idea, would you buy it? What questions would you ask of the person presenting it to you?

▶ Considering your network, ask yourself:

7) Do I have a need for networking? Do I want to be found?

8) Do I know enough people that I'm easily able to provide recommendations to friends and colleagues?

9) If I lost my job or biggest client today, do I readily have a resource that I could reach out to for finding a new job or promoting my business?

▶ Should you consider influence and reciprocity?

10) Do I know enough about the needs of people in my network to be able to effectively apply the concept of reciprocity?

11) Is my network connected?

12) Considering that you most likely cannot use reciprocity theory for every idea, is this idea worth the opportunity cost? In other words is this a time to use it, or should you save it for another, perhaps more important idea?

▶ Do you have a good idea?

13) Is it visionary, timely, and easy to understand?

14) Does it support the organization's mission, vision, and values?

15) How would you label this idea—high, medium, or low risk?

▶ Self-assess:

16) Am I being completely honest with myself or am I relating my assessment to what my behavior should be?

17) Have others commented on my behavior or skill, especially during challenging or tense circumstances?

18) What action steps can I take right now that will allow me to gain additional feedback and understanding regarding this skill, competency, or workplace behavior?

CHAPTER 3

DECISIONS AND DEBATES

"I love argument, I love debate. I don't expect anyone just to sit there and agree with me, that's not their job."

~Margaret Thatcher[1]

Making effective decisions both on and off the job is one of the most important factors of success. Of course, there is always the benefit of learning from our mistakes. Some say that failure is not the opposite of success; failure shows that you're willing to take a risk. The decisions you make, or don't make, are a critical factor in your success.

Do you love to argue? Do you love a good debate? Debates tend to create winners and losers, and for that reason alone some people love to debate. Agreeing just for the sake of keeping the peace or because it is what you believe someone wants you to do is not effective decision making. It can be difficult to go against the rest of the group, but persons who love to argue may enjoy this and even adopt a bully approach during a debate. Bullies often push for their own way.

Ideas should be challenged, and change should be encouraged. There is a delicate balance between arguing your point and creating a constructive environment that encourages new ideas, discussions, and perhaps consensus. While there may be many organizational challenges in the decision-making process, ultimately the choices should reflect the organization's mission.

Sometimes the best decision is to do nothing at all. Although it's unproductive to procrastinate, it's important to take time to fully consider an idea before making a decision. Becoming paralyzed through too much fact finding or consideration of conflicting positions may limit the effectiveness of the process. Sometimes taking too long allows groups or teams to miss opportunities that exist in narrow strategic windows.

Decisions, decisions—what will you do? And we cannot forget the boss. Love them, hate them, or love to hate them, the boss will most likely have their own ideas and anticipated outcomes from the decision-making process.

INVOLVE OTHERS IN DECISIONS

Acting on his own initiative, Jack, the director of marketing, decided to stop mailing postcards in response to customer inquiries from the website. "After all," Jack concluded in his mind, "if they are coming in from the web, they don't need a postcard. They probably don't even want that junk mail."

What Jack didn't realize is that the information technology team, who was ultimately responsible for web development, had added a check box on the webpage for clients to check if they wanted to receive postcards. Every client record being forwarded to the operations team to mail a postcard had in fact asked for the card to be sent.

This scenario and many others like it happen in organizations every day. You could certainly argue that this is about communication breakdown and it is, but it is also about decision making, problem solving, and perhaps even the organizational culture. Making good decisions in a team environment has never been more critical. We are living in a technology age; the rapid pace of information flow and exchange are almost too much to grasp. What adds to the struggle is that, due in part to the rapid change of technology, one person typically does not have the expertise or knowledge to make good business decisions alone, in a vacuum.

There is always a balance between analysis and action, especially as you carefully consider the experience and knowledge of other team members. Good, quick decisions can get a process underway, saving the organization precious time to market. The other side of this is poorer decisions that cost the organization additional resources and expense to fix. Of course, we haven't even touched on the concept of ego, pride, and organizational politics that can affect the direction of decisions and choices.

Good decisions are made when we involve others, when we strike the proper balance of experience and expertise, effective communication, and empirical evidence as we consider choices. It's important to also consider the cause of a problem before deciding how to fix it. Clearly, not solving the root cause of a problem will allow it to reoccur.

MISMANAGED AGREEMENT

"Mismanaged agreement" is a term I first learned about from the work of Professor Jerry B. Harvey, from The George Washington University, who published an article titled "The Abilene Paradox: The Management of Agreement."[2] It suggested that mismanaged agreement relates to the process or idea of agreeing to the direction or choice of a decision in a group setting, while individually, privately, not being in agreement with that choice.

Individual, team, and executive decisions can have a tremendous impact not only on other employees but also on customers, vendors, and other organization stakeholders. Mismanaged agreement is, in my opinion, one of the leading causes of unnecessary setbacks and performance failures in organizations. This idea is similar, but different from, peer pressure.

In peer pressure, individuals are pressured into changing their attitudes or beliefs to match the group norm. In mismanaged agreement, individuals disagree with a choice or direction, but openly express that they are in agreement. It is only in private that they will disclose their true feelings on the matter. They are not being honest with the group about their feelings. While there are similarities in these two concepts, the core concept is different.

Based on informal surveys I have conducted during many workshops, it seems that mismanaged agreement does in fact occur, possibly far more often than most employees would be willing to admit.

Often fear is a driving factor for those who mismanage agreement. They face the fear of separation from the group or team, or perhaps experience what are sometimes referred to as negative fantasies. These fantasies steer people into the belief that some harmful or hurtful situation may develop if they do not go along with what other group members are expressing. They fear the worst-case scenario. They do not have vision for an optimistic outcome.

STOP DEBATING DECISIONS

"A man lives by believing something: not by debating and arguing about many things."

~Thomas Carlyle[3]

Debates create winners and losers. While many people may have great interest in a good debate, including those that are on the political platforms every few years, workplace harmony will likely not begin with a debate. Someone is going to win; someone is going to lose. If you love to hate, this may excite you. If you want success in your workplace, this should alarm you.

We often face tough issues. Creating sides and dividing your organization will likely not lead to success. Successful discussions and ultimately well-supported decisions will develop by individuals building on each other's ideas. Rather than knocking down, steamrolling, laughing, or using sarcasm to quash others' ideas, you should consider building upon them.

If you have ever participated in a successful strategy or brainstorming session, a skilled facilitator probably delivered some guiding rules or principles in order to make the session a success. You have heard that no idea is a dumb idea. Don't focus too much or second guess your thoughts, just get them out there for inclusion in the list. If you build upon others' ideas during a discussion, chances are greater that you will gain buy-in.

Middle managers everywhere run around the hallowed halls whisper-shouting "win–win," and we have to have buy-in for this to be successful. They know the terms and are nearly halfway there for winning at buzz-word bingo, but sadly they are often unsure how to really create or manage buy-in. Buy-in is created through shared experiences and discussion where ideas are contributed and team members build upon the ideas or suggestions rather than debating them.

The next time you have an opportunity to discuss direction or provide input to the decision-making process, think about creating the win–win. Don't be combative with colleagues, customers, vendors, or other stakeholders. Don't debate the issues; find ways to build upon the idea. Don't love to hate; find other ways to appreciate.

GATHER APPROPRIATE INPUT

"It is intellectually dishonest to look backwards with all the facts and judge the decisions that were made with almost none of the facts, or the facts that existed hidden in the normal cloud of endless speculation of what might happen."

~Norm Coleman[4]

Attend any workshop on decision making, including one of mine, and you will learn that gathering the appropriate input is paramount to success. There exists a balance between digging too deep and not digging deep enough. However, don't let gathering information become a procrastination tool. The key to success is to gather appropriate input, to find the balance between too much, too little, and what is just right.

Who to ask, what to ask, and how to manage input is absolutely part of the process. Too often judgment and bias creep into the information flow. People who are in an emotionally charged state of mind, or who become emotionally charged as the information is gathered, are much more likely to give you information based upon bias and judgment. Not all biased or judgmental information is necessarily bad, but it needs to be effectively managed in order to make good choices.

It can sometimes be difficult to separate fact from opinion. If we are conscious of separating the two, we can easily do it; however, unconsciously, we receive input from people every day that is predominately opinion. "Go try the new restaurant down at the corner of Fourth and Main Street; they have the best food ever!" Is this a fact? No, it is an opinion. Facts and opinions get us in trouble in the workplace more often than most people realize.

Excellent researchers know how to do this right. They seek facts and empirical evidence. They often give their data the validity and reliability tests to ensure its integrity. One problem is that most of the people in your workplace (depending on where you work) probably are not highly trained researchers. Many people just go with the flow. They are inspired, influenced, or persuaded into following what sounds good. The quality of the input will condition the quality of the decision, and more importantly, the output.

MANY PEOPLE JUST GO WITH THE FLOW.

Not all decisions are best made alone, with only your own personal experiences. You can decide what you want to order for lunch from a menu, or what color of clothing you will wear to the meeting, but important personal or business choices may be best made by first gathering appropriate input.

UTILIZE DECISION BY CONSENSUS

A number of years ago I was delivering a leadership workshop to a large corporation at their worldwide headquarters. A team of approximately thirty vice president and director level participants were about to engage in a break-out activity on decision by consensus. The activity was on intellectual wilderness survival, which was designed to show the true power of decision by consensus. The whole group formed subgroups of six or seven participants. As one group assembled to my left, I overheard one of the more senior vice presidents say, "My idea of wilderness survival is a four-star hotel." Not surprisingly, this group had the poorest performance of all the subgroups.

It was not the statement that made the outcome so poor, and it was not her lack of experience with wilderness survival; it was the senior level position mixed with several more junior staff members and the authoritarian approach to problem solving. The group did not practice decision by consensus. Instead, they followed what was for them standard protocol and took direction from the senior vice president, even though she was not the best person to lead in this situation due to her self-proclaimed lack of knowledge in the subject area. Regardless, if the group had really understood the concept of decision by consensus, they would have been less likely to experience such poor performance.

Those who understand true decision by consensus realize that it is not the same as majority vote, persuasion, or authoritarian direction. True decision by consensus is often hard to obtain and in its purest form should represent all group members disclosing their logic and choice of action. When all group members fully agree, then they have obtained consensus.

In practice, decision by consensus often falls victim to persuasion or a slightly twisted form of majority vote. However, the more effective the group is at coming to consensus decisions, the better the decision or choice. I have validated this type of activity many, many times in decision making, problem solving, and critical thinking workshops. Considering this, I know based on empirical evidence that making decisions by consensus works.

IN PRACTICE, DECISION BY CONSENSUS OFTEN FALLS VICTIM TO PERSUASION OR A SLIGHTLY TWISTED FORM OF MAJORITY VOTE.

Sadly, members of committees and other groups often become victims of other problem-solving methods. Other problem-solving methods often fall short in gathering an appropriate amount of input. Occasionally I refer to this method of decision making and problem solving as being derailed by the "ivory tower syndrome," which occurs when management makes choices or decisions from their own personal agenda, feeling completely confident that they are correct. This may also be known as leadership self-deception.

False perceptions and self-deception are dangerous territory. Many leaders fall victim to blind spots and perception challenges. Evidence of these situations may be apparent in any decision-making process but are most evident in professional positions that rely on expert opinion or analysis. In some scenarios what the expert believes wholeheartedly to be truth, or even what they witness or see with their own eyes, may be different from what actually happened, or in the case of decision making, what needs to happen.

CHAPTER SUMMARY

Your workplace needs effective decision making; it needs critical thinking and excellence in problem solving. Making decisions in teams or groups by using a decision-by-consensus process is not only efficient, it is highly effective. One danger is that sometimes workplace leaders believe that getting more people involved and collecting more data slows down the process. There is truth in that concept, but the best decisions result from a proper balance of those activities.

Groups should avoid mismanaged agreement and always keep in mind that debates create winners and losers. In a healthy workplace, with a healthy team, no one should become a loser. As you consider your next moves with a decision, give thought to the following questions:

▶ When considering who should be involved:

1) Who else should be involved in this decision? Will the outcomes affect them?

2) Are data represented from facts or opinions?

3) Looking forward, what are the consequences or

drawbacks of a decision now with existing information when compared with a decision after additional research?

4) Do you have everyone involved? There is always a balance between too few and too many, but if buy-in is part of the goal, then more involvement will help broaden the buy-in.

▶ You can avoid mismanaged agreement by asking yourself:

5) What are my true feelings and experiences as they relate to this decision?

6) Am I making a choice based upon my true understanding and assessment of the situation, or am I being influenced to alter my choice based on the direction that the group appears to be heading?

7) If I am asked about this in private, would my reactions and feelings about the direction or decision be the same?

▶ Avoid debating during the decision-making process by asking yourself:

8) When the discussion or brainstorming session is over, what do I want to be different? If you are building or collecting ideas, then do just that, no decisions are necessary at this time.

9) Has a decision already been made? Sadly, sometimes a decision has already been made but organization leaders have cleverly disguised the session as a brainstorming activity.

▶ When gathering appropriate input:

10) Who has the most background or previous experience with this topic area?

11) Don't use bias as you choose individuals for input. If you have an idea of the direction you would like to go, consider obtaining input from those who would agree and those who would disagree. Who will give the most honest input?

▶ When utilizing a decision-by-consensus process:

12) Do I have all of the facts and current firsthand experience with the problem?

13) Do I have the time, support, and commitment from others to use a decision-by-consensus process for this problem?

14) Is a decision necessary at this time? A decision to do nothing is still a decision.

CHAPTER 4

DIPLOMATIC DELEGATION

"We need to accept that we won't always make the right decisions, that we'll screw up royally sometimes—understanding that failure is not the opposite of success, it's part of success."

~Arianna Huffington[1]

Delegation is easier to discuss than to implement. Leaders in nearly every capacity have some idea about the need to delegate. That is, they recognize that they should be doing it, but often allow other undisciplined actions to hold them back. When they do finally give up some of their overburdening workload, they are often so anxious about the assignment that they micromanage with an intensity far greater than required to perform the work themselves. Sadly, this often leaves them thinking, "I should just do this myself," and, "It takes too much time to hand it off to someone else." There is also a negative impact on the person being micromanaged.

Regardless of organization level, job title, or classification, delegation affects everyone in teams. Members of departments, committees, and organized task forces should be skilled at delegation.

REGARDLESS OF ORGANIZATION LEVEL, JOB TITLE, OR CLASSIFICATION, DELEGATION AFFECTS EVERYONE IN TEAMS.

Surviving ineffective delegation regardless of whether you are the hoarding supervisor or the micromanaged direct report is essential in today's economic climate. We have hoarding bosses who fear losing their job and direct reports who surf the web or play solitaire in boredom. This chapter does not entirely cover the other end of the spectrum, the end where the overzealous supervisor delegates everything and then becomes vocal about his or her accomplishments while watching the team drown in workload. While this does occasionally occur, in my experience hoarding is far more common and problematic.

DON'T COMPARE!

"Why do we get all of the work? They sit over there with nothing to do."

Have you made this or similar statements? Have you heard others make these statements?

Much like business, the stock market, and even good fortune, much of the work in any organization seems to be cyclical. The difficulty with our human senses and perception is that we tend to only recognize this when it is negatively impacting us.

Many supervisors would prefer not to face this challenge. First, how to explain it away, or second, how to effectively redistribute workloads across departments where there are opposing supervisors or skill sets and pay rates that don't align. As you are probably imagining, this can quickly turn into a nightmare, which is exactly why many supervisors turn their head and just hope to get through the whole ordeal unscathed.

Why do we compare in the first place? Much of this seems to be human nature. There are the presumed, or sometimes known, differences in pay rate, there are differing types of work, and there is what feels like the "in your face" observations.

It is difficult not to compare when you see one work group having a good time, laughing, or relaxing, when your group is scrambling to keep up with the workload. Taking this to another level, there are situations when people schedule vacations, take time off from work, or even sneak out early to coach or attend their children's sports activities. While the timing of these activities may not seem appropriate to you, your anxiety and mental anguish when comparing will not alter the outcomes.

Once upon a time there was the idea that we work for an agreed-upon pay rate, and we give 100 percent effort for that rate for the agreed upon time. Stating it in simple terms, an hour of work for an hour of pay. We've agreed on the assignment, the length of time, and the amount we will be paid. There is no need for comparison; there is no need to be troubled by what we see other people doing. We are happy and satisfied because this is what we have agreed.

On the other hand, we are human, and we will always be subject to our thoughts, feelings, emotions, and other factors that sometimes spark us into action.

While they are not always incorrect, comparisons can be unhealthy and they may make people love to hate.

Bosses who are not disciplined enough to effectively delegate will often just give the assignment to the best employee. This can create an environment where the best workers develop a feeling of getting dumped on.

Bosses notice who does the best in crisis, who will work harder, longer, and more thoroughly, and continue to give more and more assignments to these workplace stars. As the star employee looks around and compares they become angry, resentful, and may develop a love-to-hate attitude. Feeling like others are not carrying their own weight, the best workers go bad, but they don't get there on their own.

SOMEONE CAN DO IT BETTER

"Your desk is a complete disaster!" exclaimed Vince. Jason, the busy junior executive, playfully answered back with, "I can't give any of this to someone else—it would take more time to explain everything than it will for me to just do it."

People who are not effective at delegation often believe it simply takes longer to explain everything to another employee than it does for them to accomplish the task on their own. Meanwhile the pile gets deeper and deeper and the performance of the person unwilling to delegate slowly deteriorates until they find themselves handling everything in emergency mode.

This begs the question, "What are the emergencies?" Sadly, this can lead to the squeaky-wheel principle. In this principle those who make the most noise, or who are most actively pressuring someone else for their needs, are the ones who get action or get what they need.

Many organizations have employees that are not being fully utilized while other employees and supervisors are buried in work up to their eyeballs. This is true in nearly any type of organization, for-profit, non-profit, white collar, blue collar—it is everywhere.

The idea that someone else can do it better than you has merit. Not only are there likely employees that have more available time, they may even be more skilled at certain tasks. Salespeople, for example, are probably the best at closing the sale. In many cases a salesperson, account executive, or sales consultant can outsell many of the organization leaders. Honestly, they should be able to do this—it represents their job, their charge, their mission. Bosses manage; salespeople sell. It should be clear that a lack of delegation inhibits organizational effectiveness.

There will always be some work, some part of the job that only you (or your boss) can do. Chances are great, though, that someone somewhere in the organization is being underutilized. This underutilized person may possess the knowledge, skills, and abilities to perform the task more efficiently and effectively; after all, isn't that what they were hired to do?

Of course, many organizations do not have employees sitting around waiting for work to come their way. For this reason, direct reports and bosses alike need to be effective at prioritizing work. Work prioritization and effective time management skills require that employees at all levels understand the organization's mission. Understanding the mission not only gives everyone a sense of purpose, it allows them to be smart about work prioritization. While some bosses adopt the ideology of the employee works for me, they do what I say and when, sooner or later every employee with a tight schedule faces prioritization decisions.

LEAVE THE PAST BEHIND

More than a decade ago, I probed a supervisor about her unwillingness to delegate. During the conversation she repeatedly referred to a previous employer and how some of the departments shared work during the off-peak times. Then one day, a downsizing occurred. Shockwaves hit the entire organization, and suddenly it became necessary for employees to protect their work. The interest in sharing work changed.

The feeling of, "I need to be sure I have a full plate or my position will be eliminated," is a common trouble spot for employees who have experienced organizational downsizing. Their experience hints to them, if you want a job tomorrow, you have to be recognized as one of the busiest employees today.

Scars of our past should not serve as an absolute guide for our future. Sometimes we have to leave the past behind. In progressive organizations it is critical to be effective at delegation in order to rise to the next level. Any thoughts of hoarding work out of the fear of having nothing to do will create a vicious trap that you will never escape.

Fear of delegation can be deeply rooted and it plagues direct reports and bosses alike. Fear may be a factor that limits our ability to be effective at delegation. We may have the fear of separation, fear of risk, or even the fear of success.

Fear of separation can occur when a person responsible for managing a specific task feels tightly connected to a group by their involvement or contribution to that task. This fear is believed to be deeply embedded in our minds. Groups survive; the power of one is less than the power of many. If we become alienated from the group by removing ourselves as participants, we will no longer have the support of the group.

THIS FEAR IS BELIEVED TO BE DEEPLY EMBEDDED IN OUR MINDS.

Fear of risk is quickly becoming one of the most important hurdles for workplace professionals to overcome. First, we have to be sure that we are identifying real risk, and not engaging in negative fantasies about an outcome that will likely never occur. Second, real risk is a part of life. We live in a world that is rapidly changing; the riskiest position of all may be to play it safe, live in the status quo, and never take any risk.

The idea of the fear of success is different; it seems almost like an oxymoron. However, people are sometimes afraid of the responsibility or future contributions that will be expected of them should they succeed. Their self-confidence is low, and as a result they fear exposure, instead preferring to stay out of the spotlight.

They do very little to draw attention to themselves or their department. As such, they are terrible delegators and they wish to live in the safety of the status quo and moderate-to-intense workloads. They don't want the next level; they hold back. Worse yet, they hold back others in that department.

In some of these scenarios direct reports who are assertive about their career, those who are goal-oriented and highly energetic, may decide that they find little value in their job or the organization. They may develop dislike for their boss, they may even find a different passion. The passion of love to hate.

Not only is this a detriment to any progressive organization, it also may result in more employee turnover with great talent being replaced with less performance-oriented staff.

OBSESSED WITH CONTROL

According to Wikipedia, obsessive-compulsive disorder (OCD) is the fourth most common mental disorder.[2] Symptoms and diagnosis of OCD are best managed by professionals in the field of psychology or related disciplines. However, another prominent website, PsychCentral.com, lists one of many possible indicators of the disorder as: "Is reluctant to delegate tasks or to work with others unless they submit to exactly his or her way of doing things."[3] The popularity of the disorder is often the subject of jokes in many workplaces and people become inappropriately labeled as having the disorder when there has never been an official diagnosis.

Exerting too much control over anything in our lives can be problematic. This is especially true as it relates to delegation in the workplace. The inability to effectively delegate not only creates a decline in performance of the supervisor but it can also derail the performance of other employees who begin to feel discounted, disrespected, and frustrated with unsatisfying assignments.

Bosses and direct reports both need to support delegation efforts for organizational success. The boss who exerts extreme control over job tasks or work flow will need to develop the ability to let go. Direct reports can help by providing updates and feedback to the boss on a regular basis, increasing the comfort level of both parties.

This process must begin with the boss developing the willingness and ability to let go. Bosses must develop the understanding that their direct reports have, or should have, the talent and ability to take on additional assignments and job tasks. They also must recognize that as their direct reports develop into their job roles there will be developmental time, perhaps the need for mentoring, and even some errors as the learning process begins. By far, the time and effort spent on the development process is insignificant when compared with the rewards and improvements that will be obtained by the organization long term.

EVERYONE SHOULD LOOK GOOD

"Competition has been shown to be useful up to a certain point and no further, but cooperation, which is the thing we must strive for today, begins where competition leaves off."

~Franklin D. Roosevelt[4]

Unfortunately many employees have suffered the effects of supervisors dueling for power and resources for their departments. These departmental strategies often erupt when the organization is facing rapid or extensive change. It could be change due to economic slowdown or it could be change as the result of growth.

Not all internal competition is bad. It becomes harmful when it is at the expense of the organization. The organization can get hurt when competition between departments negatively affects customers and vendors or causes employees to sacrifice their integrity.

For example, internal sales teams may compete to obtain the most new accounts, revenue, or profit. Not a bad idea, but it needs to be balanced, and it can never be at the expense of valued customers and vendors. When the pressure becomes very intense, people will sometimes sacrifice their own, or the organization's, integrity.

Competition against other departments can lead to extreme delegation problems. The desire to have the biggest department, or the one that survives an economic downturn, can create numerous issues for employees. In one scenario, work volume may be extreme for one group, while the other group anxiously awaits with open arms, hoping to get some morsels of work to not only justify their existence but to eliminate absolute boredom. Boss-to-boss, department-to-department war can be absolutely brutal. Managers, owners, or others positioned in the organizational hierarchy above these departments own some of the responsibility.

The question I will often ask is, "Aren't you all in this together?" This question can cause a few moments of thought and reflection for battling bosses, but often one blames the other and the fight resumes. Much of this is reflective of organizational culture, and as previously mentioned, it is most common when the forces of change are applying pressure to the department or entire organization. This is not a plea to embrace the status quo, but recognition that as we transition through change, internal competition sometimes inappropriately thrives.

CHAPTER SUMMARY

Regardless of your role, whether boss or direct report, the tips contained in this chapter can be viewed directly as presented or considered from the other person's point of view. Often we see things differently from the other side. Effective delegation may require more empowerment, a topic that is closely related but different from delegation.

Empowerment allows the person or team who has been delegated the work the flexibility and autonomy to make responsible decisions, take appropriate risk, and feel a sense of ownership. This ownership then engages and motivates, while also providing for growth and development. High-performance employees need to feel empowered in order to be satisfied in their jobs.

▶   The next time you find yourself comparing workloads, ask yourself the following questions:

1) What do I gain from this comparison?

2) Will my observations somehow improve my performance or my job satisfaction?

3) Have I agreed to an hour of work for an hour of pay? If

yes, (and this answer is nearly always yes) then I should remain focused on my performance and not the performance of others.

▶ If you are struggling with delegation because you are not sure others can manage the task, ask yourself the following questions:

4) What represents work that *only* I can do?

5) Long term, what is the plan? Am I really going to keep doing all of this work forever?

6) Honestly assess—why am I hoarding this work?

▶ Are you haunted by the past? Do you have previous work experiences that didn't end well or were managed through tyranny and fear?

If you are the boss:

7) Is fear driving my choices as it relates to my delegation efforts?

If you are a direct report who gets limited assignments from your boss:

8) If you were the boss, what would improve your comfort level to start the delegation process moving along?

And for the boss or direct report:

9) Is the workload appropriately distributed and balanced within my department or workgroup? Are there comfort or control issues associated with the past, present, or future outlook of workflow?

▶ Could you or your boss be obsessed with control? Explore the following:

10) On any given task, is there more than one way to accomplish the work or produce the desired outcome?

11) Do I, or does my boss, allow a reasonable amount of flexibility in how the work is performed?

12) What will happen long term if the workload continues to grow and I avoid delegating because of my need to closely monitor and control this process?

▶ As an employee or boss, what can you do? Ask yourself the following questions to help find the best direction:

13) Regardless of my individual situation, what can I do to help the organization and create win–win situations?

14) Can I recall a time when the workgroups were in harmony and promoting a positive atmosphere? If yes, what has changed or what needs to change to get back on track?

CHAPTER 5

BESTOWING EMPOWERMENT

"You have to enable and empower people to make decisions independent of you. As I've learned, each person on a team is an extension of your leadership; if they feel empowered by you they will magnify your power to lead."

~Tom Ridge[1]

In my consulting practice, I am often asked by organization leaders to deliver decision-making, problem-solving, and critical-thinking training. While it is true that many employees would benefit tremendously from this type of training, often there are underlying issues causing the client to ask for this type of professional development. In some cases, employees are simply not empowered to make decisions. They may lack self-confidence, or they may not be bought-in to the organization's mission. In still other cases, they do not know or understand the mission, and as a result they cannot make effective decisions.

Delegation and empowerment tend to go hand in hand. Successful people in the workplace know and understand the dynamics of getting this right. Successful direct reports welcome and embrace new challenges and opportunities. Successful bosses recognize that they cannot do it all and be effective leaders so they readily practice both delegation and empowerment.

DISCOVER OPPORTUNITIES

"I need someone with great creative skills to work on this new flyer, but I can't wait on the marketing group to do it. Susan has this in her job description, but I can't count on her to get it finished because her skills with the software are not very good. I'll ask Beth, the receptionist. She always thrives with additional assignments, knows the software, and she'll stay late to get it finished." These and other thoughts by managers can create a breakdown in the organizational culture and promote negativity rather than motivation.

Assumptions in this scenario are that Susan is paid to do this type of work, likely a compensation package that exceeds that of Beth, the receptionist. While Beth may initially be eager, her excitement may later turn to resentment if opportunities for promotion or pay increases do not readily exist. Someone who has this task in their job description should likely already know, or obtain the skills required to use the tools necessary. While on the surface this seems to represent motivation, empowerment, and opportunity, managers sometimes need to take a longer-term or more global view of their empowerment efforts, recognizing both short and long term implications of their actions.

Managers in all sectors are guilty of this. They often look for the path of least resistance or they will bypass more senior and higher paid employees who lack the true skills but occupy space, consume oxygen, and collect a bigger paycheck. In my experience, this trend appears to be more prevalent in government and educational sectors.

IN MY EXPERIENCE, THIS TREND APPEARS TO BE MORE PREVALENT IN GOVERNMENT AND EDUCATIONAL SECTORS.

In for-profit, non-unionized businesses, job positions appear to be subject to more scrutiny and are therefore more volatile. Headcount is often connected to revenue or profit expectations based on daily, weekly or monthly goals. Simply put, job positions are held more accountable for work performed and the expense of these positions is under constant review. This scenario contrasts to other sectors where once the budget is passed you're good to go, the viability of the job position will not come in to question until the next budget cycle. In some cases, this could be one year or more.

Employees with dated skills, less motivation, and sometimes a chip on their shoulder will be left alone with minimal workload, while other more junior employees are charged with picking up the pieces which fall apart and finding alternative ways to accomplish more. All of this while these junior employees earn less, receive little recognition, perks, or opportunities for advancement.

So many possibilities are at play here. A junior employee may have more motivation when compared with those who have been in the workforce longer. Trust sometimes becomes a factor. Who does the manager trust to complete the assignment with appropriate quality and in a timely manner? Managers may choose to find another route for work flow rather than holding a more difficult employee accountable.

One of the seemingly worst abuses is when someone has the higher-level pay grade but lacks the competencies necessary for full performance. As lower-paid employees' job duties increase, their job description and compensation lag behind, meanwhile the higher-paid employee begins to accomplish less and less, measurable performance decreases, and the morale of other employees suffers.

The key to surviving this environment lies in how we view the situation. If we are the victim, we need to find something of value about this situation. We should also be cautious in our assessment to be sure that what we feel is accurate and is not being created through a false perception.

PERCEPTIONS, PERCEPTIONS

Approaching the workplace coffee station, two fellow employees notice your arrival and suddenly get quiet and walk away.

During a monthly meeting, several employees exchange glances and smiles while you are presenting your project updates.

You approach your boss's office to find one of your direct reports engaged with your boss in a closed-door conversation.

Perception is often said to be reality for the individual experiencing that situation. Perception can also cross over into paranoia and other cognitive distortions. Situations that may cause us distress in the workplace may sometimes necessitate a reality check or some other form of self-assessment. Our perceptions may be real, or they may represent an illusion based on past experiences.

Perceptions about others' work volume and their knowledge, skills, and abilities may be well founded or they may be distorted by reliving past experiences in a negative manner. Sometimes we may have the perception that we are receiving work assignments because others are under qualified or simply not capable of the assignment. In many cases we may rationalize the reasoning behind the boss's action as being caused by the boss's fear, an inability to effectively delegate, or even a desire to strike out at us with or without reason. In fact, even if our perceptions are correct, there could be positive motivators behind the boss's course of action or inaction.

Our approach to situations in the workplace can have a significant impact on the outcomes. Perceptions are natural and can help keep us safe and healthy; however, we should be cautious of snapping to quick judgments, especially if we feel threatened or angry.

GIVE YOUR BEST EFFORT

"The job pays $12.50 per hour. You will start with a forty-hour work week," stated the human resources manager.

There is a difference that often exists in our minds. We may call this attitude, motivation, or even ethics, but not everyone contributes with the same level of enthusiasm and commitment to their work. How would you react to the statement from the human resources manager—with excitement or disappointment? Of course, it may depend where we are in our career or even the current federal minimum wage. Replace $12.50 with a number reasonable for your experience or change the statement to an annual salary and benefits package. What is your mind-set? Will you give 100 percent effort or will it be something less?

We have at least two choices as we approach our work and consider our compensation package. Those of us considered to be old-school thinkers will assess the rate of pay and decide if we will accept the rate and give complete effort to that job. Others may consider the expressed rate of pay and then decide how much effort they will give based on the pay rate.

OTHERS MAY CONSIDER THE EXPRESSED RATE OF PAY AND THEN DECIDE HOW MUCH EFFORT THEY WILL GIVE BASED ON THE PAY RATE.

Many believe that an employee's approach to compensation acceptance has something to do with their age or generation. This may be true since our societal experiences and espoused values could be a predictor of workplace compensation expectations. There exists a belief that younger generation workers expect more sooner in their careers when compared to the expectations of previous generations as they entered the workforce.

Societal norms may have taught emerging workforce generations that no matter what, everyone gets the same reward or compensation. A response some believe was espoused to them by their participation in scholastic sports or academic endeavors where everyone who participated received some reward, such a trophy, plaque, or other honorable recognition.

Media and news broadcasts may also impact our perceptions of compensation fairness as they report or discuss household incomes and earning potential broadly, often with little regard to the demographics associated with those earnings. People establishing their individual value systems may be affected by their socioeconomic status and the expectations or the lack thereof from family members or friends.

Over the course of hundreds of training programs with members of several generations, I've come to believe that our approach to effort when compared with compensation is very individual. Young workers as well as those who have been in the workforce longer may have differing value systems. Self-actualization and family needs may also play a role in our work ethic and motivation as it relates to compensation. For example, some people without family responsibilities may take more career risks or accept more volatile job positions; others in that same demographic may not feel any sense of urgency to perform, since their only responsibility may be for themselves, they will simply do just enough to get by.

The difference for everyone exists in their attitude.

WEIGH THE LONG-TERM POSSIBILITIES

"My philosophy of life is that if we make up our mind what we are going to make of our lives, then work hard toward that goal, we never lose—somehow we win out."

~Ronald Reagan[2]

While taking on workplace assignments that we feel are someone else's responsibility feels like a no-win situation, we need to consider the long-term opportunities. During economic growth or downturn, often the person who is doing the work is the person who is discovered as the new leader or in the case of rightsizing, the one that must be retained. Rightsizing, a term often associated with organizations who are adjusting their workforce size due to economic conditions provides the perfect opportunity for those who have been empowered to achieve new levels of success.

Many employees are working for today. Their individual focus on the future bounces from month to month, holiday to holiday, or season to season. Many organizations have cyclical changes in performance requirements. Some experience the start of a new fiscal year, mid-year, or year-end workflow congestions. When you ask employees about their long-term goals they often seem lost for words, they are living only in the present day or at most with their sights on the next cyclical change.

We may find ourselves alarmed that at a seemingly accelerated pace another week, another month, and yes, another year has passed. Suddenly one year, three years, and five years have flashed by and we search for answers regarding the pace of our lives and the quantity of our accomplishments. This is important to remember when you may be expected and empowered to take on additional assignments or job responsibilities, even those that you are not immediately excited about.

Taking on additional responsibilities can open up many long-term possibilities for future growth. Becoming the go-to person, a trusted resource, or the organization expert has its advantages. Volumes of work mean volumes of experience. Repeatedly being asked to perform at an exceptional level may sometimes seem unfair, but when it comes to career paths it just may represent the break for which you have been waiting. Experience, whether gained or bestowed, is priceless.

REMEMBER, EXPERIENCE COUNTS!

Samantha has just graduated from a reputable college. Excited and energetic, she applies for a sales position with a well-known and growing national company. She gets an interview and is very excited about her possibilities of obtaining the position.

Mary, a seasoned sales professional without a college degree, but possessing a track record of sales success spanning over ten years, is applying for the same job. She too obtains an interview for the position. Who will the company hire?

It depends. Of course, there are many possibilities to consider for this scenario. There are many opportunities for those with experience. Some fields or occupations require college degrees, such as the medical profession or legal practice. Other occupations rely more heavily on background or experience rather than a college degree, such as in trade skills or sales. Debates continue about the value and return on investment as it relates to a college education, but the general rule of thumb has been that a college degree is always better than no college degree. My point is that it really all depends, but you should never underestimate the power of experience.

Experience, like any education or training, cannot really be taken away from you. If you have some college credits or an entire degree, plus experience, it is the best of both worlds. As we obtain employment early in our careers, we may encounter opportunities for experience. Often experience, like a college degree, has associated costs. Costs may include the expense of working at a lower rate of pay, doing similar or the same work as seasoned professionals. We have at least two mind-set choices here: 1) be disgruntled and avoid the opportunity, or 2) welcome the opportunity, seeing it as a stepping stone for the future.

There are many other variables involved here, but the moral of this story is that experience counts and often there are opportunities that we may or may not take depending on our mind-set. The next time you find yourself taking on assignments where other employees should or could be doing the work while you feel taken advantage of, consider what future opportunities or experiences you may be able to create.

THE RIGHT JOB

Susanne slapped the alarm clock beside her bed to stop the onslaught of its annoying sound. A new day was starting, but that meant just another day at work. Susanne was not excited about going to work today, or any other day for the past six months.

She doesn't feel engaged in her work and often feels like she lacks the true connection required to be successful in this position. Socially, she gets anxious and angry when someone asks her about her job or what she does for a living. Her job satisfaction is very low and she doesn't have trust in many of her coworkers and the management team. Often feeling burnt out, she only stays in this job because she doesn't want to look for a new one. Susanne may be underemployed or simply not empowered to work at a level comparable to her true potential.

Susanne is probably not in the right job. Maybe the problem is her place of employment or it could be the business sector or worse, her career path. The choices we make can drastically affect not only our workplace life, but our life outside of work as well. Many choices exist for job changes, although economic conditions can impair our ability to find options during extremely turbulent times. A business acquaintance once suggested that there are always jobs available; the question is where do you want to live? Many people have family ties and commitments to certain locations; they find themselves attached because of children, schools, and homes.

THE CHOICES WE MAKE CAN DRASTICALLY AFFECT NOT ONLY OUR WORKPLACE LIFE, BUT OUR LIFE OUTSIDE OF WORK AS WELL.

In simplest terms, we have two choices, we can go or we can stay. Going for most people means finding a new employer and staying means that we have to find a way to cope with our existing situation. The variables and parameters of these two choices are dynamic and different for every situation. Susanne, as the example illustrates, probably needs to find a new job. Your personal situation may not require a new job, but perhaps a different way of managing your perceptions and attitudes toward your employer.

Career-minded professionals often have a need to be empowered as they continue to reach for more, if their boss or place of employment does not provide this opportunity for growth and continued development, the employee will likely become very dissatisfied. Lack of action to rectify this situation can affect not only the morale and contributions of one employee, but this image may spread to other employees or even outside of the organization to customers, vendors or other stakeholders. A costly situation that no organization can afford.

Organizations must have the right people in the right job. Employees must share in this responsibility by adapting or moving on. Do you love your job, or do you love to hate the boss?

BEING UNDEREMPLOYED IS NOT AN OPTION

Dave spent about six years working in a successful family business after graduating from high school. A downturn in the economy and increased competition forced Dave to consider his options. He enrolled in a small local college and began working toward a bachelor's degree as a non-traditional student. Dave excelled in business and management classes, having already established a great deal of knowledge in these areas from his work experiences. Working and going to school created additional challenges, but after another six years, Dave graduated with honors from college. He sent resumes to potential employers with businesses a reasonable commute from his home. After several interviews, he was offered an entry-level position with one employer. It was not directly related to his work experience or his degree, but it did position him to move beyond the struggling family business.

Your job, your career, your family life, and downtime may feel difficult to balance. Knowing the right steps to take and when to take them seems to require a crystal ball. The feeling of being underemployed can be devastating and it can be the precursor for a variety of negative and harmful workplace outcomes.

Underemployment[3] may include any scenario where the compensation or work performed is something less than what it should be when compared to a personal standard. For example, if an employee was a manager for ten years and for some reason takes a different job in a similar field where the level of responsibility and compensation package represent only a fraction of the levels previously earned, that person may be considered to be underemployed.

While every situation and scenario is different, it is important for each individual to find an appropriate balance. There are risks and costs associated with nearly every decision you make. Making good job and career choices are not exempt from this category. You may be very happily employed. You may be in a situation where nearly any job is a good choice because of personal financial meltdown, or you may be seeking to advance your career, or even change careers while already being adequately employed. Every person needs to weigh carefully both short- and long-term goals as well as the proper balance for downtime, for friends, and for family.

Being underemployed may be about your attitude toward your work or career. The long-term costs of an underemployed attitude, whether real or imaginary, can be devastating. Underemployment for extended periods of time can take its toll not only on your resume but in your personal life. Are you underemployed?

MIX IT UP

Sitting at her desk, Lisa feels extremely unmotivated. It is only the middle of the morning during her normal daily nine-to-five job. It isn't the afternoon slowdown, not enough caffeine, or that she is a lazy professional. Tedious and repetitious work that doesn't provide any challenge and lessens her feeling of professional competence is in part the cause. Bored, she scans her immediate environment and opts for a walk to the restroom and coffee station. Passing several offices and work areas she notices more life and a feverish hustle and bustle from other staff. In her mind she asks herself, "Am I getting all the ridiculous, mundane, and uninspiring tasks?"

She is not alone. Many workplace professionals, regardless of their career path, field of work, gender, or age, sometimes ask themselves similar questions. Everyone has moments of feeling disconnected, disengaged, and bored in the workplace. If this feeling is so overwhelming day after day after day, it may be time to consider some self-assessment and new options.

Often we begin this type of self-assessment process by observing the work practices, flow, or volume of activity others in similar positions are experiencing. This assessment can be valuable not from the standpoint of judging the ease, skill, or enjoyment of their tasks, but from understanding what other opportunities may exist for you to expand your horizons and grow within the organization.

Reflection and observation may lead to new discoveries of how to make your work more interesting and, better yet, how to get more of it. Time goes by very fast when we are extremely busy or otherwise preoccupied with tasks other than checking the clock. If your work feels tedious, repetitious, and mundane it may be that you need either more volume or more challenge. Assess your workplace to spot tasks that are being neglected by others or that others can't keep up with. Additionally you may be able to spot opportunities to learn more about the organization or play a bigger role in adding value to other processes or products. You may find an opportunity to be more productive and valuable, rather than feeling unmotivated and disengaged.

THE BIG PICTURE

Mark just left another meeting with his boss. Assignments, projects, and his normal daily workload sometimes don't align with his career goals. Frustrations with his boss have him second-guessing his value to the organization. At the same time, he's curious whether his boss has something bigger planned for him in the future. At times his workload feels loaded with duties that are beneath his competency level, yet he often feels part of the future during visionary and strategy discussions.

Many professionals are very career minded. While many people fall short on their three- or five-year career plan, they know that they are working toward something greater. When they feel job assignments are not supporting the values that they envision for their future, they often become frustrated and in many cases start to analyze the occurrences of assignments they don't enjoy rather than strategizing on how their overall contribution is adding value to the organization.

Many managers place higher value on the employee who will jump in and get the job done as compared to those employees who are uninterested in organizational goals and more interested in personal goals. This alone is enough to make you think twice about your role and ultimately what will yield the most positive results for your future. Many of the most successful employees strategize and take actions that will support their futures with the organization. While some seemingly do this out of common sense, others have a more specific game plan in mind.

Setting goals for the future of your career is not as difficult as actually making them happen, but often people procrastinate about the goal-setting process and simply skip planning altogether. One of the keys to successful goal setting is to consider realistically where you want to be in three or five years and then develop a road map toward achieving that goal. We tend to focus on past short-comings, errors, and mistakes, when instead we should be focusing on positive contributions we have made and how we can align our natural talents and interests with opportunities in our current workplace or the path we visualize for our future.

BE THE TRUSTED RESOURCE

Jerry, a very accomplished executive whose track record of professional achievements would stand toe-to-toe with the best in his field, needs to delegate some very critical administrative work. This work is high priority and needed to be finished yesterday. Jerry struggles momentarily, not knowing the best place to hand off this mission-critical work. Technically, it is an assignment that is appropriate for one of the entry-level clerical employees, but Jerry needs to have confidence that the work will be completed to a high standard. Jerry gives the assignment to his top administrative assistant.

This scenario is all too real for many workplace professionals. We could dissect the paragraph above and create discussion points from several different management angles including proper delegation, people management, and even hiring practices; but the point in this case is finding the positive in Jerry's delegation opportunity.

The administrative assistant who received this work may feel discounted, disrespected, and used. This assignment, based on the described scenario, is beneath her normal capabilities. Why would the boss give her this assignment when there is a more junior person who is quite capable (when held to an appropriate standard) of performing this task? For Jerry, this administrative assistant is the trusted resource.

THIS ASSIGNMENT, BASED ON THE DESCRIBED SCENARIO, IS BENEATH HER NORMAL CAPABILITIES.

Being the trusted resource may not always feel like the most glamorous job and it may test your patience and commitment to the organization. After all, from this point of view, you have just been dumped on. You may ask questions such as, "Why me? Why not someone else?" and "What did I do wrong that I deserve this?" In fact, your high level of performance has positioned you to be the go-to person for seemingly simple assignments that require the highest standards. You are the trusted resource.

You could argue many different positions, one being that if you do entry-level work your market value or earnings potential will decrease. Another could be that it is a waste of organization resources, that a person earning much less in salary and benefits should be quite capable of this assignment. Yet another position could be that the entry-level employees do not receive the work because they are not held accountable. However, being the trusted resource does have its benefits. The next time you feel trapped or devalued by being assigned to work that may feel beneath you, think again.

CHAPTER SUMMARY

Empowerment is an interesting topic that sometimes relates to delegation, or lack thereof. While empowerment may be conditioned somewhat by your boss, it may also be something that you can tactfully encourage. Individuals in the workplace can self-manage various situations that ultimately create opportunities to learn, grow, and become more valuable. Empowerment may be very apparent, or may be something you have to draw out of your current circumstances. Unbalanced levels of empowerment may make you love to hate the boss.

► To discover opportunities, ask yourself the following:

1) When doing the additional assignments, are my job skills improving, making me more valuable?

2) Would I be happier if someone else were asked to do it, or do I crave the responsibility and would simply appreciate some recognition and appropriate compensation?

3) Is my assessment or perception of this situation correct?

▶ Help clarify your perceptions about work assignments and other employees' contributions by asking yourself the following questions:

4) Is it my job to examine the work contributions of other team members? Would my time be better spent focusing on my workload without examining others?

5) What are the employee classifications, rank, and salary differences? Perceptions of unfair distribution of workloads may be amplified or elevated by position or length of employment, technical skills or a lack of those skills, and the employee compensation and benefits system. Self-assess your contributions and your own knowledge, skills, and abilities.

6) We all have choices; we may face challenging and difficult situations but it may also be our choice to stay or to leave. What positives can you find in this situation? (Some positive views may include saving jobs, perhaps your own, during economic challenges or building new skills and helping others succeed.)

▶ Are you giving your best effort? Consider your approach to your job and the compensation and benefits package as you review the following questions:

7) Pretending I am now the boss, business owner, or the person otherwise responsible for the oversight of this job, what would I expect?

8) Will the organization recognize me based more on my work ethic and contributions, or will my job be evaluated based on my compensation (costs to the organization)?

9) What are the long-term benefits to both me and the organization if I am truly focused and committed to delivering my best effort?

▶ As you consider long-term possibilities to enhance your knowledge, skills, and abilities by working through workplace challenges, ask yourself the following:

10) What opportunities may emerge as I expand my knowledge and experience?

11) Where do I see myself in three years or five years? Have I planned a course for my career beyond my present-day role?

12) What experience beyond the obvious is obtainable by assuming added job functions, duties, or responsibilities?

▶ Your experience counts. Ask yourself the following questions:

13) Setting aside any negative feelings toward the situation, how can I use this situation to my advantage?

14) How might this experience add to my skills, professional resume, or support my educational

background and complement my other life or workplace experiences?

15) If I were an outside observer of my situation, what might I want to say about the opportunity for this experience and my future career?

▶ Are you in the right job? Answer these questions to help you decide:

16) Do you feel disconnected, unappreciated, devalued, and disrespected? Do you feel drained, tired, and exhausted with the emotional climate in your job?

17) Do you feel that you are constantly getting dumped on, receiving the worst tasks or projects? Do you struggle to find anything good, rewarding, or gratifying about your work?

18) Do you have a higher than normal level of mistrust with your immediate coworkers, your supervisor, or other team and management members?

If you have answered yes to two or more of these questions (16, 17, or 18) it may be time to consider another place of employment. If that is undesirable or otherwise impossible, you will need to use coping strategies that help you remain emotionally healthy during your time spent in this position.

▶   Are you underemployed? Consider your reactions to the following questions to help you decide:

19) Do you feel capable of intellectual work or technical job skills above and beyond the scope of your current job role or job description? Do you feel overqualified or overeducated for your current job role?

20) Is your compensation package appropriate for the work that you perform (realistically)? Is it comparable with other similar jobs in your field and in your geographical area?

21) Are you frequently bored with your work? Do you see opportunities that you would like to explore but cannot because of other job role responsibilities?

▶   Are you bored with your work? The next time you are bored at work ask yourself the following questions:

22) Can I take on additional assignments? What are they, where are they, and how can I get appropriately involved?

23) If I ask my supervisor for additional work, what will happen? Will showing initiative improve not only my personal outlook but also better position me for future opportunities?

24) What can I do to think about my current role and workload from a new perspective? Where are my contributions most valuable and how do they fit into the big picture?

▶ Here are several questions to ask yourself when attempting to align your job or career goals with the big picture:

25) What are my natural talents, and how do they align with my current role and future opportunities?

26) How do my talents, interests, education, and experience align with what the organization needs? (Focus on looking at it from the organization's perspective, rather than your own.)

27) After analyzing my career goals, how can I communicate with my boss or other organization leaders to start the process moving forward?

▶ Sometimes being the trusted resource means that you are called upon by the boss to do tasks that you feel are beneath you. It sometimes feels like disrespect, but is it? Are you a trusted resource? Ask yourself the following questions:

28) Will this assignment increase my exposure to other key managers, executives, or top-rated clients?

29) What can I learn about this situation or the core competencies of the organization by doing this work?

30) Becoming the go-to person sometimes has benefits. Will this increase my long-term value to the organization?

Dennis E. Gilbert

CHAPTER 6

DRESS FOR SUCCESS

"You cannot climb the ladder of success dressed in the costume of failure."

~Zig Ziglar[1]

I learn a lot about disgruntled employees from clients. I hear about the lack of motivation, the difficulty in finding loyal employees, and about fights regarding the dress code. Dress codes vary greatly from manufacturing environments to health care to service organizations. In some businesses it is very clear, or at least clearer, than others. If you are an automotive mechanic you are probably not going to try to, or be expected to, wear a business suit to work. If you work in food processing or some type of refrigerated production facility, wearing skimpy clothing is probably not a good idea. In many other cases, dress code is not so clear.

Dress code issues seem to be more common among female employees than male employees and in offices more than in manufacturing plants. It does not seem to matter so much about age, job role, or years of service. From senior executives to the lowest-ranking employees, I hear a lot about dress code.

If you work in human resources, you have heard a lot about dress code. If you have an employee handbook, the pages related to dress code are probably tattered and torn from frequent use. If it is an online handbook, it likely ranks in the top three of section searches. Dress code—it's a big deal.

JOB PERFORMANCE

"Wear a suit and tie for the meeting tomorrow."

"I would suggest slacks instead of a short skirt."

Employers spend a great amount of time managing or attempting to manage the dress code. Frustrated, shocked, and confused supervisors and direct reports alike often choose to simply look the other way rather than face the conflict associated with complaints or misunderstandings about the dress code. This often results in selective choices on who gets the talk and who does not. Many managers choose to deliver the talk to those whom they believe will handle it the best and meanwhile they claim to not notice other offenders. As you may imagine, this topic could quickly spread into so many areas from perception to safety to discrimination.

Considering what is appropriate for the climate, the job role, and the type of business or organization may just scratch the surface. After spending a few years, from the mid-1980s through current day, in professional office environments, I do have a small collection of stories. If addressing an employee's attire is performance related it would seem reasonable that we should focus on the type of business, the climate and weather conditions, and personal comfort.

Personal comfort is an area where things sometimes start to go wrong. The definition of personal comfort can be broad. Some people feel shorts and a bright Hawaiian shirt may be cool and make them feel comfortable while meeting with the executives from the corporate office in Miami. "This makes me feel comfortable," they may exclaim. The reality is that unless the meeting is being held at the beach or poolside bar, it may not be appropriate.

If we are meeting with bankers, lawyers, or professional business executives, both men and women cannot go wrong with professional dress. If we focus on the performance of the job, or the nature of work, adapting to that environment typically means falling in line and blending in with the norms. Realistically, this is where the most performance-oriented benefit comes from. If everyone is comfortable that the dress code is being followed, then everyone focuses on job performance not dress code.

REALISTICALLY, THIS IS WHERE THE MOST PERFORMANCE-ORIENTED BENEFIT COMES FROM.

Dress code is a challenging topic and the best success stories with managing it seem to stem from the idea of job performance trumping all (reasonable) opinions of proper dress. Employees who blend in and adapt to the norm would appear to make everyone more comfortable and should allow more focus on the job.

SEXUALLY APPROPRIATE

"Your top shows too much cleavage," proclaimed one woman in a disgusted tone to another.

This and many other similar comments related to skirt length, shoes, or even how snug a particular clothing item may fit are commonplace in professional office environments everywhere. It is not limited to a specific gender with discussions and comments frequently emerging about waist size, the muffin top[2] (waist line body fat hanging over the top of pants), and even buttocks of both male and female employees.

People learn, and those people in society who have experienced a positive reaction to their physical appearance (sexual prowess) will typically do one of two things. First, they will either exploit their features in an attempt to positively influence others, or second, they will shy away from such features, trying to hide or minimize any potential effects. Dressing for a job interview may find the applicant facing this kind of personal decision making.

Everyday attire in the workplace for both male and female employees should be environmentally neutral, seasonally appropriate, and not too revealing. For clarity, environmentally neutral represents being appropriate for the type of work or the workplace environment, which in some cases could represent a uniform. A chef should wear chef's clothing, a mechanic may perhaps wear overalls, and your financial advisor in a business suit would seem to make sense. Seasonally appropriate means long pants as opposed to shorts if you are in climatic conditions where the temperature easily dips below freezing and not too revealing for the ladies means skirt lengths that are probably closer to the knees rather than hips, and conservative tops would mean no mid-riff showing and limited cleavage exposure.

Even as you read these words variations of the rules are bound to cross your mind, including the idea of what I think versus what someone else thinks and so on. Most of us can pass good judgment on circumstances where or when something is too little or too much. Again we learn and recognize from past experience when our clothing may have been inappropriate. The rub to all of this starts to develop as we consider people who want to stretch the boundaries or use their attractive physical features in an inappropriate manner to obtain consent, control, or even a job promotion!

DON'T BE JEALOUS

"Jealously is, I think, the worst of all faults because it makes a victim of both parties."

~Gene Tierney[3]

A good friend of mine who has worked in the human resources field for many years believes that some employees are "petty, vindictive, and gossipy" and she also strongly believes that those traits are more common in female rather than male employees. I invite you to use your imagination to consider the countless number of scenarios that may occur in any workplace environment.

I would like to focus on how you can reduce or eliminate the struggles that you sometimes face with dress code and the idea of envy or jealously. One of the first is to recognize that this is in fact, sometimes an issue. My experience from the numerous complaints I received while serving in managerial roles in small to mid-size organizations is that while envy and jealously play a significant role, people rarely admit it. Many believe that if you remove the jealously and judgment the problem is gone.

Not exactly though. For some people, the problem is not judging or jealousy, but envy. But wait, it is not that they are envious of what's under the hood; it is that this other person can get away with provocative dress. So in some cases the envy comes not from the idea that they wish they had the physical characteristics to support the outfit, it comes from the idea that the other person has the guts to do it and worse yet, management looks the other way. Management simply doesn't see the problem, or they refuse to do something about it.

Consider that there are at least three camps. The first camp has envy, jealously, and judgment of others based on the idea that they don't have the physical prowess to wear more suggestive or provocative clothing. The second camp at a minimum has envy, but they choose to not wear clothing that is more revealing, suggestive, or otherwise inappropriate, because it just wouldn't be the right thing to do.

Both of these camps likely have a problem with efficiency, productivity, and their attitude. They waste time gossiping and are often emotionally distracted from their work. They share their ideas with others trying to create buy-in or find acceptance and confirmation for their distress. Dress code is creating additional problems for them.

The better camp is the third camp. The third camp is the, "I don't care what others are wearing I am focusing on my job" camp. This is the camp that bosses like. Perhaps mostly because they do not have to deal with the dress code issue, but also because this camp is more efficient, productive, and more performance focused. Just a guess, but I think there is a better chance you love to hate the boss if you pitch your tent in camp one or camp two.

TEST THE RULES

Sherry works in a fast-paced office environment but very seldom has any face-to-face contact with customers. During the warmer summer months her office area tends to overheat. The climate control in her office area is marginal, and it seems like it is always too hot in the summer and too cold during the winter. She notices that several women are wearing sleeveless tops, short skirts or Capri pants, and flip-flops or sandals. The office dress code does not support this attire, and every day she expends energy complaining and withdrawing with envy that the other women get away with this.

Sherry feels trapped. She simply wants justice. She asks herself every morning, "How can these women get away with not following the dress code?" It doesn't stop there. She takes inventory by walking around the office to observe how others are dressing. Normally a very conscientious worker who always follows the rules, she is frustrated and feels a lack of respect for her supervisor and the organization. Sherry feels more and more disengaged every day. She blames the boss for not taking what she considers to be appropriate action. Her feelings are starting to shift, she is starting to love to hate the boss.

The best possible scenario for Sherry is to focus on her own work, her fulfillment of her job duties and responsibilities, and simply to be as productive as possible. If that isn't possible, perhaps Sherry should consider altering her dress to take advantage of some of the bending of rules occurring in her office. After all, the age old adage "if you can't beat them, join them" just may have some positive outcomes in this scenario.

Rules are not meant to be broken, and in its purest form I would never suggest that someone purposely break the rules. Dress code rules are tough. There are so many opinions on what is right, what is wrong, what should be acceptable, what is comfortable, and the possibilities for disagreement and argument are nearly endless. What I would like to suggest is that in many scenarios there is some wiggle room surrounding dress code and in cases outside of required uniforms or safety concerns the dress code is normally put in place to uphold the image of the organization. For example, in a professional (white collar) business, men should wear business suits and ties, women, business slacks or business dresses.

In this case the biggest rule that may need to be broken is Sherry's own rule of being the highly conscientious worker who is as black and white as the pages of this book.

WHY DO YOU CARE?

"Sometimes the questions are complicated and the answers are simple."

~Dr. Seuss[4]

Dress codes are a delicate matter. Many people struggle with dress codes every day, not from the perspective of what to wear but from the perspective that they believe others are getting away with something that they so strongly desire. As this chapter explored the concepts of job performance, sexuality, envy, and jealously, all of which are related to most organizations' dress codes, I hope it has stimulated your thoughts for deeper understanding and reflection.

So, why do you care? Not about your workplace, or your coworkers, your boss, or direct reports, but why do you care so much about the dress code? In the big picture of your life, why does this matter so much? Sometimes we have to let go; we have to drop our beliefs and value systems to conform to standards that may not be consistent with our system. Just because we wouldn't do it, doesn't necessarily mean it is wrong; it may simply mean that it is different.

Being different isn't always bad, in fact in some cases it exemplifies leadership. Acceptance of difference is also a quality that can be embraced through leadership. People come to work for different reasons. For some, their work is their career, to others it is something that they must do to earn a living and beyond the pay per hour and collecting their paycheck, they really don't care a lot about work.

FOR SOME, THEIR WORK IS THEIR CAREER, TO OTHERS IT IS SOMETHING THAT THEY MUST DO TO EARN A LIVING AND BEYOND THE PAY PER HOUR AND COLLECTING THEIR PAYCHECK, THEY REALLY DON'T CARE A LOT ABOUT WORK.

I believe that although some people will never fall in love with their work or career it is important to engage and be part of something. Worrying less about what someone is wearing and paying more attention to productivity and organizational mission is likely more important. One could argue that not following the dress code is insubordination and evidence of a non-team player. Perhaps, but then again being different isn't always bad.

The answer here seems simple. If the attire of any employee does not infringe on the values of the organization and it does not affect safety and it does not directly affect you—why do you care? Stop loving to hate.

CHAPTER SUMMARY

Dress code is one of the most common areas that sparks the feeling of loving to hate the boss. Employees struggling with dress code issues typically turn the responsibility of managing compliance back to the boss. Of course, the boss has responsibilities here, but harmonious organizations have fewer dress code issues when compared with organizations that are experiencing higher negativity and harmful conflict disturbances. Whenever I've asked about dress code, professionals from all levels and sectors have laughed, complained, or empathized over the problems associated with dress codes in the workplace.

If you have read this chapter in its entirety you may have found your anxiety increasing, some of the issues mentioned are challenging and often mismanaged. I believe it is important to consider whether all the fuss about dress code is really worth it. Agonizing, gossiping, and wasting time doesn't seem positive or beneficial in any way. Outside of safety issues, cleanliness, and nudity; does what someone is wearing really matter that much? Debrief with the following questions:

▶ Before you jump out of your skin with outrage the next time you see something inappropriate, ask yourself the following:

1) Am I dressed in accordance with the norm?

2) How does this dress code situation or this person impact my personal job performance? How should it, or shouldn't it?

3) What is more valuable to me, my time and energy spent on the violator or my time and energy as it relates to performing my job?

▶ Are you dressing appropriately? Are you conforming to your workplace standards and guidelines? Ask yourself the following:

4) Am I taking advantage of physical appearance strengths appropriately without causing discomfort to others? (This is a balancing act; don't hide, but don't overexpose.)

5) Appropriately self-assess by asking, would my mother, father, school teacher, pastor, priest, grandmother, grandfather, or the Pope feel that what I am about to wear is too revealing or too risky?

▶ Feeling a little outrage about the clothing someone else is wearing? Ask yourself this:

6) Does their clothing directly affect my work or in any way (other than my mental state) affect my job performance?

7) Does their clothing represent an image or a reputation of the organization at large, that as a result I do not wish to be part of the organization? (Or is it personal preference and not directly related to the image of the organization?)

8) If you are not offended but feel envy because you would like to dress differently, have you explored those options?

▶ If you have considered testing the rules, begin by asking yourself the following questions:

9) What is the worst-case scenario if I bend the dress code rule slightly?

▶ Do you find yourself caring too much about the dress code? Let's see:

10) Is my ability to concentrate and focus on my work impacted by the attire of other people? (Not my feelings about their attire, but their actual attire.)

11) Is the future of my success or my career somehow in jeopardy because of the attire of someone I work with?

12) Does worrying or becoming upset about someone else's attire positively impact my mood or the outcomes of my day?

Dennis E. Gilbert

.

CHAPTER 7

OVERLOOKED FOR ADVANCEMENT

"I believe that it's better to be looked over than it is to be overlooked."

~Mae West[1]

Talent is everywhere. Finding it, capturing it, and appreciating it is often more difficult. Some would quickly agree that putting warm bodies into workplace positions is easy, especially during times of high unemployment. Putting warm bodies with the appropriate knowledge, skills, and abilities into positions is much more challenging. Finding great talent, the appropriate talent, is difficult.

Through my best guess, I believe that at least 40 percent of the active workforce feels that their true talent, their knowledge, skills, and abilities have either been underused or overlooked all together. Argue this best guess as you see fit, but so many of my clients discuss this topic with me that I believe I am conservative in my estimation.

Getting noticed is sometimes the problem. We may have difficulty getting noticed because of timing, or our ability to sell ourselves. Many people feel overlooked. When you consider position advancement, in many cases there are more employees in a department or workgroup than there are positions for advancement. In simple terms, for every five or ten employees there may be one supervisor or other leadership role. Acquiring this role is not everyone's goal, but often there is more interest than there are available positions. This simple fact makes being promoted much more challenging than just being average.

MAKE SURE THAT YOUR HEART IS IN IT

"Did you see the new job posting for the manager of large accounts?" asked Susan. Her enthusiasm and interest outshined many recent reflections of her engagement in the workplace. Was Susan really interested in the job, or just surprised at the posting and the thought of a more advanced position? "I'm thinking I may apply. I don't know, what do I have to lose?" she went on to state. Susan may be suffering from the Moderate Interest Fear of Failure (MIFF) "syndrome" and she may become MIFFed if this opportunity does not work out. Do you think Susan will get the job?

Looking at this through an appreciative inquiry[2] lens could possibly suggest that Susan is not envisioning or co-constructing her future. She is missing out on the dream and design phase of the appreciative inquiry model.

Job markets are pretty challenging, especially during an economic slowdown or recession. The number of unemployed workers when compared with the number of job openings is not favorable. In addition, finding the job that stimulates you, engages you, and advances your career can be even more challenging. In other words, if you are already employed, finding another job is one thing, finding your dream job may be tougher.

The dream and design phase of the appreciative inquiry model would suggest that you dream, fantasize, think big, without limits, about the job you want and then you design your next move, your future, your career around that dream. This is a great approach to discovering what really moves you, being positive about the possibilities and outcomes, and designing a path that will lead to your success.

Susan may lack the initiative and motivation required to get the job managing large accounts. Her half-hearted, moderate approach will likely show in a lack of enthusiasm and energy while crafting a cover letter or worse yet could show up during a job interview should she make it beyond the initial resume scan by the hiring committee.

Have you ever been in Susan's position? Most people who have been in the workforce for at least five years have explored some type of job change. People in the workforce much longer or those who are exceptionally ambitious could have encountered a similar dilemma many times. There are many reasons we go forward half-heartedly. It could be a lack of true interest or it may represent other emotional challenges. Depression, paranoia, or even just a lack of self-confidence may allow us to apply, but not be successful, only adding to our list of disappointments and shortcomings. Being positive and remaining positive is often a reflection of our past experiences.

Having a long-range goal for a rewarding and positive disposition in the workplace may be determined by choices that we make during our career. Failure to obtain a new or better position can feel devastating, but it shouldn't. Trying something and failing is not the worst thing. If you are performance oriented and wish to accomplish more in your career, the worst thing is thinking about it, considering it, and deciding up front it is beyond your reach. What is worse? You settle for less.

MAKE SURE YOU ARE REASONABLY QUALIFIED

Often after a workshop, a small percentage of participants will approach the facilitator to ask a private question. In my experience, questions vary depending mostly on the workshop content but occasionally individuals are seeking some direction or validation of a thought or feeling as it relates to career path and their individual professional development.

During my career, at this point spanning more than twenty-five years, I have encountered three types of attitudes of individuals actively seeking a job change (not those simply wishing for a change). The attitudes are under confident, overconfident, and well balanced. Needless to say, the well-balanced attitude is most likely the best approach, although depending on your personality and qualifications you could make an argument for one of the other approaches depending on the circumstances or situation.

A well-balanced attitude would imply that you are humble enough to accept advice and consider input from various resources, while also not coming across as arrogant, cocky, and above the work or people in your target job market. With under confidence, you use language or words that indicate you lack the confidence or ability; over-confident and you may talk down or demonstrate an attitude that the work is beneath you. The balanced approach sends the message that you don't know it all, but you are interested, qualified, and a fast and eager learner.

When approaching any new job opportunity, we should reflect on our true qualifications for the job. This is where accurate self-assessment continues to play a role in our ability to pursue job or career changes. Assessing your true qualifications for a new position is one of the most important steps in the pursuit. There is a difference between having to reach or stretch for qualification justification and simply not being qualified.

Some of this depends on our level of confidence and some of it depends on reality. For example, stating that you are confident you can sell cars because you have previously been in a sales role and your hobby is restoring old cars is probably reasonable. Stating that you can sell cars when you have never been in a sales position, never had a driver's license, and don't know the difference between an automatic transmission and a manual transmission would likely indicate you are not qualified.

Comparably speaking, an associate degree in psychology does not make you a psycho-therapist. The ability to hang a picture on the wall does not make you a carpenter, and a part-time job in a assisted living facility does not make you a nurse or emergency medical technician.

Being self-confident is important, being overly or inappropriately confident can be a disaster. In our careers, our self-confidence tends to develop based on small wins. We take some risk, we take a chance, we learn from success and failures, and ultimately develop more, and hopefully not less, self-confidence. Appropriate confidence is important as we self-assess our qualifications for a job.

THERE IS A DIFFERENCE BETWEEN HAVING TO REACH OR STRETCH FOR QUALIFICATION JUSTIFICATION AND SIMPLY NOT BEING QUALIFIED.

Pursuing a job or career change can be a pivotal moment in anyone's life. It forces you to consider who you really are, what risks you are willing to take, and if you are prepared for the commitment and responsibility associated with such a change. Are you qualified for the next step?

BE CREDIBLE

A speeding red convertible slows for the traffic light at a busy intersection, the light turns red, the car pauses but proceeds to make a right-hand turn into traffic that has started to move from the other direction. Two cars collide; no one is seriously hurt but the cars are unable to be moved from the scene. Standing at the corner, a middle-aged man is witness to the accident. He is not clean shaven, his clothes are ragged and dirty, and he is pushing a shopping cart apparently filled with his only possessions. Police arrive at the scene and ask if there are any witnesses. Will the man standing at the corner be considered a credible witness?

In the workplace we are likely not representing the image of the man on the corner and we could evaluate this story to include so many societal biases it could fill a chapter in this book; however, it serves as an analogy to help illustrate credibility.

Credibility is often attributed to those who are in apposition of power. As the saying goes, it may be "yours to lose." Credibility in your job role relates to how believable or trustworthy you appear to others. Many argue that credibility and respect, once lost, is very difficult to regain. Some employees may not view you as credible or respect you upfront; it may have to be earned. The process of obtaining credibility can take time.

When you consider pursuing a new job you may want to consider if you are credible. Just as in an accident or crime scene people may seek a credible witness, in the job market, potential employers seek credible people to fill job openings. Candidates' resumes, education, work experience, and even their appearance will play a role in their credibility.

Being credible in the workplace means that you are believable, you are trustworthy, and you are a good fit for the job position that you either hold or are pursuing.

Judgment on whether you are, or are not credible often sits in the hands of your future boss or the hiring committee. If you don't believe in yourself, if you don't look, act, and carry yourself as being credible, strangers or those who you are meeting for the first time will likely not believe in you either.

Those who are seeking a job promotion within their existing organization may be subject to opinions or memories of past experiences by those responsible for awarding the promotion. This is where your on the job attitude, accomplishments, and your network will sometimes come into play. They may review previous performance evaluations, your human resource file, and informally ask co-workers about your skills or likability. They may pass appropriate, or inappropriate judgment and you may be evaluated based on character or the perception of value that you hold in your existing role. They will decide if you are credible.

INFLUENCE YOUR VISIBILITY

Rhonda and Stephanie work side by side every day. Both have been with the organization for nearly three years and both have similar experience and educational backgrounds. Both provide administrative support to a busy office staff of nearly thirty employees. They are about the same age.

Nearly identical when it comes to their workplace profile, there is at least one significant difference. Stephanie seems more popular with the other staff members and often serves as the distribution point for work assignments, which are then mutually agreed upon and balanced between the two employees. She is more visible.

Visibility may be created in many ways. People who are more vocal, frequently volunteer, ask questions, and even those who are well dressed may be viewed as more visible in a workplace setting. Individuals who are more visible typically receive more call-to-action requests, are the first to be picked for teams or committees, and are the first to receive credit for job performance.

PEOPLE WHO ARE MORE VOCAL, FREQUENTLY VOLUNTEER, ASK QUESTIONS, AND EVEN THOSE WHO ARE WELL DRESSED MAY BE VIEWED AS MORE VISIBLE IN A WORKPLACE SETTING.

High visibility does not mean that you are credible, but it does increase the chance that you will be recognized for your efforts. In contrast, low visibility may mean that your contributions, regardless of the effort you extend, may go unnoticed. Unfortunately, someone who is more visible may inappropriately receive credit for shared

LOVE TO HATE THE BOSS

accomplishments. All hope is not lost; those who desire to become more visible can change their situation.

Influencing your visibility is not difficult, but in some cases it may cause discomfort. Individuals who are uncomfortable with being more vocal about their accomplishments will struggle with influencing their visibility. Those who are highly visible are successful at self-promotion. They are not hiding, not ashamed; they are self-confident and recognize that there is a proper balance between no promotion and excessive bragging. Individuals who think negatively about self-promotion do not sell themselves; instead they tend to sell others, harming not only their own visibility but in some cases their credibility. There is a proper balance, and popular wisdom would suggest that successful people strike a healthy balance.

BECOME VISIBLE!

"My track record is impeccable, I have the experience and the education required, but I continue to be overlooked for advancement opportunities," stated Susan, a mid-level manager in a small but growing technology firm. "Worse yet, I am starting to feel like my direct reports don't respect me anymore. I think they are aware of my desire to move up and that I'm not being recognized as a candidate," continued Susan.

Susan is definitely not alone. Stories like hers abound in corporate America, and from many other sectors including government and non-profits.

Perfect attendance, strong annual performance evaluations, and outstanding credibility are not the only factors for advancement. Building strong workplace relationships can also have a tremendous impact on individuals being recognized for promotions or job changes. Additionally, an individual's visibility can play a significant role.

Visibility in the workplace means that you are not only seen, but you are also heard. Highly visible employees, including those with less than stellar performance records, may have built the relationships that count when it comes to job changes or promotions. This is often referred to as workplace politics.

Reluctance to play in the political undercurrents eliminates what I will estimate at 50 percent of the job pool. Many highly qualified candidates never get to the interview stage, let alone become a finalist for the position. Some individuals write themselves off before even giving it a chance by telling themselves that employees are promoted through the buddy system or that their workplace is a "who knows who" environment. Some of this may have validity, but how can you become part of this elite pool?

Individuals need to be more than credible; they need to also be visible. Highly visible people seize opportunities as they present themselves. Speaking up in meetings, attending extracurricular functions and events, volunteering, and even dressing for success will improve your visibility.

Before meetings, do your homework. What is one possible solution to a pending challenge that you can bring to the table? Network, get involved in activities, join a committee, offer helpful verbal contributions, get noticed. Becoming more visible is not really difficult for most otherwise successful employees; they just have to apply themselves and take the risk to get noticed.

STAY TRUE TO HIGH QUALITY, HIGH OUTPUT VALUES

"Every dog has its day!"

Perhaps nothing can zap our workplace energy more than the thought of someone else reaping our hard-earned rewards. In addition to the monetary rewards we receive for coming to work every day and doing our job, we all, to some extent, are motivated by acknowledgement from others and feeling a sense of achievement or accomplishment. Most of us take pride in the work that we do. This pride is what causes us to flinch or withdraw when we receive feedback that suggests we need to improve our performance.

So many arguments exist for who is to blame for lack of acknowledgement or appropriate credit being given for workplace accomplishments. Arguments exist for rewarding and acknowledging the entire team, highlighting individual achievements, and saying very little with the thought being it is what was expected.

For example, if the team reaches or exceeds the monthly goals should they be rewarded as a team, or individually? If they are rewarded only as the team (an important concept), the top performers in the team may feel some disappointment. This disappointment can lead to resentment with the top performers deciding that they will contribute less. For them, there becomes no point in excelling, everyone is rewarded the same.

Here is the point, if you have a team of twelve people, do all of them contribute or perform equally? Probably not, and as such you will have star or top performers, average performers, and those who may be fully performing (meaning they shouldn't be fired) but are only doing just enough to get by.

Effective bosses find ways to strike a balance between team performance and individual performance. If you are a boss and you have the attitude that the team did what was expected and as a result no praise, feedback, or acknowledgment is necessary, you may have some challenges ahead. You should probably think twice about that approach.

Feedback on our performance can lead to higher output and greater achievements or it may derail performance and zap the necessary energy or commitment to excel. Sometimes we blame the boss and the boss sometimes blames the staff. Blaming others is not a productive step toward curbing any anger or resolving the issues and problems. If you are guilty of the blame game, you need to stop blaming others and refocus your energy.

While we cannot necessarily control what others do, and we cannot always control who receives the credit for workplace efforts, we can choose our own attitude. Attitudes are contagious, and if you seek the positive in people and workplace teams you can help to make a good attitude a viral experience.

By taking what is sometimes called the high road approach, you can continue to give your best effort in even the most difficult situations. Making a difference for the organization is always a good idea. Staying true to yourself and remaining energized to deliver all of your tasks and assignments with high quality and high output will make a difference for you in your organization.

MAKE YOUR PERFORMANCE COUNT

Your boss was just promoted—additional responsibilities, higher salary, and even a new, bigger office. The view from that floor of the building must be pretty impressive. Unsuspecting and unaware, you notice a press release on the corporate website listing her recent promotion. Her list of accomplishments contains the project that you worked on tirelessly for months! You feel devastated; you loved that project and you are proud of that accomplishment. The credit for your work has been stolen.

This scenario and many others like it are far too common in our workplaces today. Many people believe there has been a cultural shift and that having multiple generations in our workplace today may play a role. People who have been in the workforce longer may adapt readily to an authoritarian approach. They may believe that their only value is to serve the betterment of their team, their boss, or the entire organization. Others feel quite differently. They know that the future of their success lies in their own hands and after all, their individual contribution is what will make the difference.

MANY PEOPLE BELIEVE THERE HAS BEEN A CULTURAL SHIFT AND THAT HAVING MULTIPLE GENERATIONS IN OUR WORKPLACE TODAY MAY PLAY A ROLE.

In reality, while multiple workforce generations may cause some challenges, it is not appropriate to stereotype all persons within a specific generation to behaviors that are largely represented by that group. In other words, not every person who has been in the workforce for thirty years does not embrace technology and likewise not every person entering the workforce in their late teens or early twenties lacks work ethic and just wants everything handed to them.

I happen to believe that contributions are what make the difference, and evaluation or critique of others should be on an individual and case-by-case basis. Certainly stereotyping an individual or group of individuals and applying a label to them does not necessarily make them more prone or less prone to effective performance in the workplace.

Someone taking credit for your work can happen in any sector and by nearly any employee. If you face this challenge you may be tempted to go on the attack. You may make a quick decision about what to do and how to react out of anger.

While an aggressive approach may feel comforting during the heat of the moment, the long-term consequences should be considered. After all, your reputation and respect are still on the line, and the appearance of an overreaction is probably not a desirable outcome.

Instead, focus your energy on future projects that provide you with challenge and opportunities for both personal and professional growth. Making your performance count during this time is critical. Supporting and embracing your boss remains important since changes in your boss's job role may invite more opportunities for your future.

Stop loving to hate and redirect your energy toward a better future!

BALANCE PERFORMANCE WITH REWARDS

Andy just had his best month in sales results since joining the business nearly one year ago. His boss took a risk when hiring him since Andy had no previous sales experience. Not only was Andy excelling in his sales role, his boss was also just recognized as a top performer for their region, which covered a three-state area. Andy contemplated his future with the organization. On one hand, things were great and he was excelling. On the other hand, his boss was also benefiting from the results of Andy's effort. Andy started to resent the fact that his boss was achieving newfound success based on the increased sales.

Andy and his boss both face one of the toughest workplace challenges. How do they properly manage and balance risk, performance, and reward? Even the best organizations struggle with striking the proper balance. Andy has grown during his year of employment and his boss, who took a risk when hiring him, has also grown. Everyone is winning, but Andy is growing impatient.

All organizations should first consider their individual policies and procedures related to jobs, job descriptions, and compensation packages. Establishing up front, guidelines, expectations, and to the extent possible, future opportunities, will help to minimize negative conflict. Beyond the hopefully obvious scenario of aligning this situation to the predetermined policies and procedures, Andy and his boss should engage in a private conversation to establish the basis not only of future expectations, but also future rewards.

What are the options here? Often our ability to see the options affects our ability to solve the problem. There are two sides to this story. The boss took a risk, Andy has good performance, the boss is recognized, and Andy begins to get resentful. If you are the boss, you probably believe all is well. If you are Andy, you are looking for additional rewards, and you may feel the organization and your boss are coming up short. Success for both parties in this situation will necessitate finding the balance between performance and reward. Are you being appropriately noticed and rewarded?

CREATE OPTIONS THAT GET YOU NOTICED

"Setting goals is the first step in turning the invisible into the visible."

~Tony Robbins[3]

It is no secret that setting goals helps you to keep on track and measure your progress. When it comes to improving your visibility, one of the first steps is to discover your options. We all have options. Failure to see the options is what holds many people back from accomplishing what they desire. When you consider the need to improve your visibility, the options are sometimes driven by your goals.

This chapter has focused on the executable action items to help change your destiny when someone else appears to be getting the credit for your work or your accomplishments. Visibility can be controlled. It can be minimized or maximized and it may be scaled anywhere in between. Leaving your comfort zone may represent the first step in becoming more visible. Many employees have put walls around themselves in an effort to not draw attention. Some believe that bringing attention to yourself may be the first step in self-destruction and that includes attention garnering actions during slow economic times when management may be looking to cut positions.

LEAVING YOUR COMFORT ZONE MAY REPRESENT THE FIRST STEP IN BECOMING MORE VISIBLE.

High-performing organizations embrace those who get results. Every job may have a different set of expectations and performance measurement criteria, but most positions within organizations today are not created as a luxurious place for rest and relaxation while also being paid. If you are the employee of a high-performance organization, you need to get noticed. You need to take creative actions that generate opportunities that get you noticed.

Options that get you noticed are often presented as opportunities. Some of us take them, and some of us do not. In small organizations this might mean offering to do many different tasks in a wide variety of areas. Smaller organizations typically lack the people resources or diverse talent pools required for all tasks. If you are talented in a way that can help your organization, speak up, ask questions, and offer assistance.

Larger organizations, which are typically very departmentalized, will often not have a wide variety of opportunities, but opportunities still exist. If you are in a larger organization, look for committees, social affairs, and sponsored training activities that you're interested in and get involved.

In either situation, small or large organization, if you don't want to be overlooked, you have to be willing to get noticed.

CHAPTER SUMMARY

Talent is everywhere. Based on my experience and informal comments from many workplace professionals, I believe a very large segment of the active workforce believes that they have been overlooked for advancement. Certainly in some cases this is true, but in many other cases it may not be true.

Self-assessment is critical when considering who you are and what your options should be. Some claim to want additional responsibility and the higher wage that goes with it, while others are happy right where they are. In still other cases, people in the workforce may complain about big wage earnings out of envy or jealously while they clearly lack the knowledge, skills, and abilities to perform at that level.

If you are still reading this chapter, I trust that career advancement is either important to you now or you are curious about what makes the difference for some and not others. Before casting any blame toward the organization or the boss, consider asking yourself the following questions as you assess your position on being overlooked for advancement.

▶ Is your heart in it? Before applying for that next job consider the following questions:

1) Am I truly interested in this job, and am I willing to accept the additional commitment and responsibilities?

2) Assuming I successfully obtain the position, can I visualize myself as fully performing in this role?

3) Do I meet or exceed the minimum qualifications, and can I demonstrate the knowledge, skills, and abilities required?

▶ Are you qualified? Ask yourself these questions before applying for the position:

4) Am I being realistic in my assessment of this opportunity?

5) Can I express through my resume reasonable qualifications for the job?

6) Assuming I make it to the interview stage, will I be considered credible?

▶ Are you credible? Consider these questions to help evaluate your credibility:

7) Do I demonstrate confidence in my job role and duties?

8) Do others in my work group or team trust me? Does my boss trust me?

9) Am I visible? Are my contributions noticed?

▶ Interested in influencing your visibility? Consider the following:

10) Do I attend gatherings, meetings, and other events that provide opportunity for more exposure?

11) Am I appropriately vocal? Do I ask questions and offer at least one interaction in group settings?

12) Do I volunteer for work assignments, dress professionally, and initiate conversations?

▶ Becoming more visible? All employees should ask themselves these visibility questions:

13) What are my opportunities to become more visible?

14) Do I strive to build successful workplace relationships? Am I well networked?

▶ In an effort to stay true to high-quality and high-output values, even when recognition for working with those values is minimal or non-existent, you can make a difference by asking yourself the following questions:

15) Would I want any perceptions of my performance to be less? In other words, if you pull back and stop delivering high performance the likely outcome will be even less visibility for your achievements. In scenarios where you feel like your output is not valued and workers with less commitment and effort get the same or more recognition, pulling back and not giving your complete effort is most likely a mistake.

16) How does my attitude influence the outcome?

17) Maintaining a positive approach, what tasks or activities can I perform to help improve visibility?

▶   When making your performance count, ask yourself the following:

18) Does your boss ever take the credit for your work? If asked about the contribution to the project or work, what might the boss say?

19) If your boss takes credit for your work and you are considering confronting him or her, first ask, when the conversation is over, what do I want to be, or what will be different?

20) Size up this situation. Are the outcomes of a confrontation worth it? Is this the right circumstance and the right time to make a stand?

▶   When trying to balance performance with rewards, ask yourself the following questions:

21) Play mediator. What is really going on here? Is it financial, is it ego, is it both—or something else?

22) What are the measurable expectations of the boss or the organization? Perhaps more importantly, what should they be?

23) Role play both sides in your mind. What are the short- and long-term risks, performance expectations, and rewards? Is the situation balanced?

▶   Having an acute awareness of your visibility and creating a plan is the first step to getting noticed for advancement opportunities. Here are a few questions to consider as you formulate your plan:

24) Have you honestly self-assessed? Do you know where your knowledge, skills, and abilities can make the most impact?

25) How will you balance your visibility plan? Spreading yourself too thin by volunteering or making commitments that you cannot uphold would be devastating.

26) What is your timeline? If your needs are very urgent, you need to make choices that will provide immediate impact.

Dennis E. Gilbert

CHAPTER 8

YOU'RE NOT MY BOSS

"There is only one boss. The customer. And he can fire everybody in the company from the chairman on down, simply by spending his money somewhere else."

~Sam Walton[1]

It makes sense that the customer is the boss. But after the customer, who is the boss?

In the mid-1980s, I moved to Lancaster County, Pennsylvania, and lived there for about one year. Upon first arriving, I spent a few weeks with my sister before finding a home to rent. My nephew, who was about three or four years old at the time, was intrigued with the visit from his uncle. I forget the details, but during one particular interaction, I corrected him for something that he did or did not do. Quickly he responded with what I remember as a boyish lisp, "You're not the boss of me, Uncle Dennis!" He quickly grew away from that innocence and today is an outstanding young man with a family of his own, but I still recall my playful jabs at him where I would ask him, "Who is the boss?"

Power struggles, lack of respect, and misunderstood organization charts are at the top of the list when it comes to workplace problems and identification of the boss. There are those who have more than one boss and then there are those who are employed in a small family-owned business. In the case of family, regardless of any rank, family members are almost always the boss. In other words, if you are employed in a family business and your are not a member of the family, any family member of any rank in the organization may be someone to regard as the boss. There are boards of directors who are the boss, and there are those who for reasons unknown are sometimes the boss.

If you love to hate the boss, chances are good your situation is somehow covered in the preceding paragraph. The first step in facing challenges of determining the boss in a particular situation is to understand the powerful dynamics at work in these situations.

POLITICAL POWER PLAYS

Barbara and James, both long-term employees of the same corporation, were advised that they were being considered for a job promotion. Based entirely on observation, other employees would consider them to be close friends because they often share morning coffee, visit each other's offices, and even enjoy the occasional after-work cocktail. The stakes have now changed, and the younger and more vulnerable James is about to go on the ride of his life. Sadly, he is blindly unaware.

Barbara's approach to achieving the position is to privately, secretively, make James look bad. She lacks the self-confidence for a clean fight. She has little desire for long hours but enjoys looking successful among friends while avoiding discussions that may expose her incompetence.

James's approach is to work hard, stick to the facts, and demonstrate his worthiness by bringing forward empirical data to justify his opinions and vision for the more advanced position.

Long story short, James prevailed. Over several months, the board of directors (responsible for the decision) became aware of the political power play being executed by Barbara. In fact, they had figured this out long before James. Barbara didn't play fair. She gained support of many direct reports and staff by attempting to highlight the shortcomings of her rival. A move the board didn't respect and could not trust. After all, what if she decided to sell them out, or even worse, the organization.

James, on the other hand, ignorant to Barbara's dreadful and demeaning ways, trudged on each and every day. He worked from his heart; his approach was honest and straightforward. The board believed in James and not only was he qualified for the role, he demonstrated tremendous integrity and was well respected for his commitment to direct reports and team efforts. Qualities the board admired for a leadership position. He was the successful candidate, no thanks to Barbara's efforts to inappropriately crush her competition.

HE WORKED FROM HIS HEART; HIS APPROACH WAS HONEST AND STRAIGHTFORWARD.

People sometimes do strange things. Even immoral or unethical behavior is not out of the question when it comes to ego validation, image, and workplace survival. We often hear stories of scandal and white-collar crime on the news. My experience has shown me that if you give a salesperson a quota and if they feel that they have no options, some of them will do nearly anything to maintain their employment.

Worse still, in smaller privately held organizations, some business owners thrive on bringing on those who have not experienced personal success. Insecure and lacking self-confidence, some business owners prey on desperate people, giving them enough hope and rope to do what they say or simply hang themselves. Like observing laboratory animals, they watch from a distance with a grin in their soul. If you believe in karma or the negative consequences of those who sacrifice integrity and ethics to get where they are going, then you are a person who needs to develop a keen sense of awareness for these villains and ignore their political power play while you are on your way to success!

DON'T LIVE THE FANTASY

"The disappearance of a sense of responsibility is the most far-reaching consequence of submission to authority."

~Stanley Milgram[2]

Some people promote themselves; they make up their mind that they are authority figures in the workgroup or department. Chances are good that someone recently suggested to them that they are not assertive enough to get a promotion or else they just came back from the boss's office and somehow misread the conversation and now they believe they are in charge. When I worked in academia we used the acronym B.M.O.C. to describe this. Appropriate for males or females, it stands for Big Man On Campus.

Getting along in the workplace is critical for workplace success. We need to be able to effectively communicate, have reasonable levels of trust, and be able to sense the needs and emotions of others. I am certainly not going to suggest that we fight with our coworkers about who is in charge, and in many cases who is in charge may not matter all that much. What I will suggest is that we are smart about our interactions with others, especially when those others may single-handedly decide to take on the role of authority. Simply put, people like this will act like they are your boss and you are their servant. Even the real boss should not approach working with you in this manner.

Sadly, this is another workplace reality, this concept of others behaving in an authoritarian manner and expressing or attempting to demonstrate that they are in charge! Some people may roll with this concept and let power grabbers have their way, others will sit on the fence, and others might fight back with unsupportive behavior. The person who has chosen to become the authority sometimes falls under a different guise—the bully.

You don't have to live the bully's fantasy. In fact, there are many drawbacks to allowing that fantasy to become your reality, including actually becoming the bully's direct report.

Make no mistake, this is a delicate situation and the spirit of teamwork and your organization's mission must maintain top consideration as you deploy your defense.

AVOID EMOTIONAL TRAPS

The battle among direct reports and bosses can be fierce. The battle among those who lack formal power but who relish the next power move and those they attempt to overpower can be devastating. Unclear lines of authority, inappropriate relationships, and called-in favors can wreak havoc on workplace productivity, morale, and employee loyalty.

UNCLEAR LINES OF AUTHORITY, INAPPROPRIATE RELATIONSHIPS, AND CALLED-IN FAVORS CAN WREAK HAVOC ON WORKPLACE PRODUCTIVITY, MORALE, AND EMPLOYEE LOYALTY.

Emotional conflicts with your boss or those who want to pretend they are your boss can sabotage your entire career. Sometimes I feel like I have seen it or heard it all, then bam, I'm hit with a new surprise. I've heard of purposely throwing away mail, intercepting telephone calls, planting or withholding information, scanning e-mail accounts and hard drives. People will sometimes do surprising things, especially when they feel the stakes are high.

People in the workplace with an inappropriate mission may look for weaknesses in others. They may keep a low profile, launching subtle little digs here and there in an ongoing effort to derail their nemesis. Emotions can boil over quickly and easily, especially during times when there are other workplace stressors. A challenging economy, shortcomings on sales goals or revenue projections, funding cuts, government or technology changes—all can represent additional stress throughout any organization.

Remember that you have choices and that often, even unconsciously, you may contribute to the existence of challenging workplace relationships. You may have to set boundaries with coworkers. You may have to step up, confront, and resolve the challenges that others impose. Most importantly, avoidance or doing nothing will likely result in more of the same. There are exceptions, but ultimately you can decide. You can take appropriate action and risk or suffer the consequences and constraints of the continued emotional traps.

LOSE–WIN

Nearly everyone knows and understands the concept of a win–win. Simply put, it means that in situations of collaboration, not just one party is benefiting, both or all parties are finding some benefit. While many understand the win–win, they do not so readily understanding the other possible outcomes. Sometimes people set themselves up for a lose–win. They take a position that lessens their credibility, lessens their value, and welcomes disrespect.

Don't create a lose–win for your job role. Don't take the back seat. Don't approach conversations and opportunities with the idea that you are less; approach those opportunities with the mind-set that it is your turn to shine. You've waited patiently, and now is your time.

What is your role? What do you want it to be? Sometimes we create our job role. Many supervisors and human resource professionals will honestly tell you that there is the job description, and then there is what the person in that job really does.

Of course, I'm not suggesting that job descriptions are purposely inaccurate or not valuable, in fact, I would argue the complete opposite, but in many cases they are a starting point, or a guide. Short of strict union jobs, the job description in smaller private firms often serves as a starting point or a record of what is expected. Such descriptions are probably similar to what appeared on the help-wanted advertisement.

The person who fills the position may shift some of those job duties and responsibilities based on their knowledge, skills, and abilities. To some degree, they make the job unique to them. The organization benefits from the true talents and the work performed may shift slightly from person to person, even when they may have the exact same job description.

Don't set yourself up for the lose–win. Strive to understand your value and the qualities that you bring to your job role. Seek to contribute fully as a team player and not to get caught up in performance-robbing emotional conflicts with those who want to be or who try to be your boss.

CHAPTER SUMMARY

Being the boss may be desirable to some, frowned upon by others. Some people try desperately to live out their fantasy in the workplace. Of course, conceptually this is not all bad, but when it is at the expense of others or when it is handled inappropriately, it can be sickening.

If you are career and goal minded, someone trying to be your boss without the formal power or authority can quickly make you love to hate. We have to watch for politics in the workplace, be cautious that we don't get caught up in someone else's fantasy, and always be striving to create the win–win, not setting ourselves up for the lose–win approach.

▶ If you believe you are a puppet in a political power play, consider asking yourself these three questions:

1) What is the high-integrity, ethically responsible approach for you in your particular situation?

2) When considering your options, what behavior will have the best long-term outcomes for you?

3) If you do nothing, that is, you stay focused on the job at hand and your job description, what will be the outcome?

▶ If you don't want to live someone else's fantasy, here are a few things to think about:

4) If you do nothing, what will happen?

5) Are you contributing to this problem? An example would be making sarcastic jokes or granting someone authority beyond your understanding of his or her job role.

6) Sometimes the direction we should take is clearer from the back, rather than the front. Being overly assertive may not be the answer. Sometimes taking the time to observe and be more calculated in our approach will help us see miscalculations and wrong turns. When the time comes to take action we are then better prepared. Consider your approach carefully, if you are in this situation would a slower, more calculated approach be more productive?

▶ Emotional traps can be devastating. Consider this:

7) Have you felt your emotions boil over at work?

8) What is the end result if you let your emotions get the best of you?

9) Can you feel your emotions starting to boil? Learn to recognize the early warning signs and shut down any emotional outbursts before you make a big mistake.

▶ Don't set yourself up for a lose–win.

10) Are you appropriately self-confident?

11) What have you been successful at in the past?

12) How can you build on your previous success?

CHAPTER 9

SOME IN THE FAMILY

"He wants his son to follow in his footprints."

~Archie Bunker, *All in the Family*[1]

All in the Family was a popular sitcom during the 1970s.[2] If you've seen this show, then you may be smiling as this chapter begins. This television show was not about the workplace, at least not specifically, but it did demonstrate a variety of circumstances related to family matters, acceptance or lack of for someone outside of the family, and the conflict that may be associated with people needing to get along with each other. Lead character Archie, who played a politically conservative, working-class bigot, certainly threw out some jokes about work, life, and family here and there.

Archie was never graceful with his words. He often was angry, but well intended. He wanted to sound intelligent and well educated, but he would make up words and phrases that sometimes rhymed or had a true meaning different from his expression. Such is the case with the opening quote in this chapter. Of course, what Archie intended to say was, "He wants his son to follow in his *footsteps.*"

Many businesses, but especially small ones, can struggle with family matters and the workplace. These struggles can range from the small business owner going through a divorce and having the spouse tear apart the business financially, to family members scattered throughout organizational levels creating stress and strain on other employees and supervisors, to being entirely family owned and operated facing challenges on budgets, planning, and incomes.

Family in business can be fantastic but it can also be very challenging. As you may already realize from personal experience or the horror stories you've heard from friends, family owned and operated businesses that also hire others outside of the family may have additional struggles.

DOUBLE STUFFED

"Who's the kid with the Oreo cookie?"

~Oreo slogan, circa 1986[3]

If you were over the age of five in 1986, you may be able to hear a cute little jingle bouncing around in your head from the Oreo cookie commercials. "Who's the kid with the Oreo cookie?" was broadcast widely through both television and radio. They are great cookies and those are great memories for some. Today many flavors of the cookie exist, and there is even a variety of the cookie that they label, double stuffed. This idea of being stuffed in the middle, sandwiched in between two other objects, draws an analogy to working in a business with a variety of family members working at different organizational levels.

Being sandwiched between the big boss and an employee who is a relative of the big boss can be an unpleasant experience. Most common in small businesses, especially common in small family-owned businesses, family members may span the organization chart. I've personally heard many grievances from workplace supervisors who are struggling with a workplace family challenge.

The challenge may start out with some background information like this: "The company owner hired his sister's son to work on the plant floor, and I am the plant-floor supervisor." This scenario and perhaps hundreds of other variations are commonplace in many small businesses.

The challenge for the supervisor in this situation is how to effectively and appropriately manage this employee. In many cases, these situations do not cause problems. If everyone does their part and does not abuse or disrespect the system, it may be okay. In other cases, this may invite, encourage, and otherwise create a love-to-hate-the-boss scenario.

Imagine the possibilities. The big boss talks shop with his nephew at Thanksgiving dinner and hears that all the plant employees hate the plant-floor supervisor. In another example, the plant-floor supervisor might be responsible for providing a performance review for the big boss's nephew—a review that in honesty would not be so favorable. Have you witnessed this or something similar? Are you one of the characters in any of these scenarios?

FREE LABOR

Richard has run a successful business for twenty years. He started the business with a friend who is now deceased and the business has become quite successful in the past few years. It has become his enterprise, his domain. What started out as just a couple of entrepreneurs with an idea has grown to just over sixty employees. Richard's son Ken has recently graduated from college and rumor has it that he barely made it through; however; he is now a manager in the business.

At a quick glance, the business appears to be flourishing, revenues are increasing, and profit margins remain steady. The employee headcount seems nearly correct and employees are busy, but occasionally hit some slow times for a couple of days. Many employees are grateful for their jobs and the business success in an otherwise struggling economy.

MANY EMPLOYEES ARE GRATEFUL FOR THEIR JOBS AND THE BUSINESS SUCCESS IN AN OTHERWISE STRUGGLING ECONOMY.

Ken just bought an old farm estate in the country, which is somewhat modest when compared with "Dad's place," but still costs much more than the average employee would be able to afford. Ken, on the advice of his father, has kept a fairly low profile about the purchase of the home. Some of Ken's direct reports are well aware of his home and all come to the understanding that the family business will take care of family, and although they are not part of the family they remain thankful for the opportunity and for their jobs.

During a slow week at the business, Ken is anxious to get some work around the old farm finished. A few slow days at work provide great opportunity. Ken selects three of his best guys to head out to the farm to help out. They are on payroll during this time. "After all, they are being paid by the business," Ken thinks to himself, "they may as well help out." They jump in their pickup trucks and off they go.

Is there a problem here? Some would argue yes, and others may say no. Would a situation like this affect employee morale and loyalty? What other aspects of employee engagement, respect, and organizational commitment may be affected? Many organizational development experts would quickly identify some problems here. While the problems may not be legal issues, and they may not be safety issues, or even directly involve others in the workplace, there are substantial "no-no's" happening.

Consider the employee who has been waiting patiently on a raise, a raise that perhaps has not occurred because of a tough economy. Consider the employee with some maintenance issues at their home that they have not had the chance to address, either financially or with time constraints. Then there is the single mom, she is a supervisor, and has wanted to attend her daughter's soccer match out of town but cannot because she would need to leave work early to make it. She cannot leave early because her department is short staffed with some of the employees helping out at Ken's farm.

Are you seeing some patterns or trends here? The family can't understand why the employees are not as committed as they once were. Hiring family may be one thing, managing your business and your personal life by utilizing business resources is another.

FIRE FIGHT

"I don't even like firing people. I don't think I've ever said, 'You're fired' to anybody."

~Martha Stewart[4]

When you are in business and you have family involved in your business it can feel wonderful, like a great accomplishment. Perhaps there is a sense of pride in creating a destiny that includes members of your family. Life is good—until someone is not holding up his or her end of the bargain. Firing anyone can be tough. Firing a family member, well, that can be disastrous.

FIRING A FAMILY MEMBER, WELL, THAT CAN BE DISASTROUS.

There are businesses with many workers, some of which include family. There are businesses that are made up entirely of family, and there are businesses that are not family owned and operated but that employ various members of a family. In all of these cases, things can work out, and in all of these cases, sometimes things don't work out.

Sometimes a situation arises in family businesses where someone should be fired and is not, or someone who doesn't deserve to be fired may be fired to set an example. If you have experienced trouble with family in business, you have probably loved to hate the boss.

Many people believe that you should not hire family. The idea is to keep it simple and clean, protect and enhance the morale of employees, and prevent any future family issues. Granted, a no-tolerance policy has its advantages, but like many policies there often are exceptions, especially if it is a very small business and tough economic conditions exist.

The golden rule, if one exists, is to try to remove the emotional connections from these decisions. When it comes to family not only can that be difficult, but it can also cause hard feelings outside of the workplace.

When hiring family members it is important to state some ground rules. The ground rules should apply to family as well as non-family employees. If family members do not expect special treatment and the ground rules are laid out appropriately up front it can work. Many people are employed in businesses where this is working.

My experience tells me that it takes special care and in-depth understanding from all employees of the boss's intent for fairness, likewise the boss needs to stick to policy, procedure, and be extremely fair. Employees will always be on the lookout for the boss being too forgiving or too harsh to both family or non-family alike.

What would you do? If you are a business owner, manager, or otherwise in a capacity to hire and fire family members would you, do you?

CHAPTER SUMMARY

Every workplace has challenges. Workplaces with family members employed have some additional challenges. There may be both benefits and drawbacks to family in the workplace. What one organization faces as a challenge could perhaps be strength in another. Family members may bond together, stick together, and fight the good fight to achieve even greater success. Sometimes with new levels of success there develops new challenges.

Many businesses will continue to achieve great levels of success both with and without family being employed, but one constant will develop in most—someone will love to hate the boss.

▶ If you are stuffed in between family members on the organization chart and are struggling with employee performance problems, ask yourself the following:

1) What will happen if I do nothing? Will the situation deteriorate further or will it remain about the same?

2) How critical is the situation I'm facing related to my own job performance?

3) What would happen if I appropriately follow the chain of command and make an attempt to openly discuss my discomfort with the situation?

▶ Are you struggling with business resources being used for personal gain in the family business? Ask yourself the following:

4) What can I do to change this situation? Are there options?

5) Is this situation negatively impacting my ability to grow and develop my career?

6) Do I feel a sense of commitment and loyalty from the organization? Should I be committed and loyal?

▶ Does someone need to be fired? Pretend for a moment you are an outside observer. Consider the following:

7) In a family-owned business, an employee who is also a family member is abusing policy and procedure to the extent that if they were not family, they would have already been fired. Should the business let this person go?

8) A small business with family scattered across various layers of the organization has a family member employed in a middle management capacity. There are various

performance-related problems with this family member, and more importantly other employees are claiming favoritism. Employee morale is at an all-time low, apparently a direct result of this situation. The family would perhaps be more tolerant if this wasn't a family member but they feel they need to set an example and fire this person—should they?

CHAPTER 10

BEING A SIRIUS PERFORMER

"The true measure of the value of any business leader and manager is performance."

~Brian Tracy[1]

I love a good pun. Sirius, of course, is a star. It is known as the brightest star in the sky visible from Earth. Are you a star performer? Star performers have a significant impact on the outputs from any organization. Workplace stars or exemplary performers are measured by understanding both high performance and low performance as a rating among a group of individuals. If we cannot measure or recognize differences in performance within a group, then we could never identify the stars. While this seems to be stating the obvious, I am often asked how organizations determine or categorize stars, average performers, fully performing, and those needing to be removed from the organization.

It may be helpful to provide some definitions. Stars are the top performers, they represent the ideal employee. Average performers are probably the largest segment or population, they do a good job, but they are really just average. Fully performing employees represent the group that is below average, they perform but only minimally, typically just enough to keep them from being fired. The final group, if another group exists, represents those employees who should be removed from the organization.

This chapter is important for everyone who is a star, everyone who wants to be star, and everyone who is not a star. This chapter is for everyone. Bosses and direct reports alike should be interested in understanding more about themselves and about what drives or limits the performance of others.

EXPECTING MORE FROM OTHERS

"You begin by always expecting good things to happen."

~Tom Hopkins[2]

We face at least two approaches to life at work. First, we can be optimistic and positive, looking for and making good things happen. Or second, we can be the pessimist, see the glass as half empty, and have negative fantasies about opportunities gone wrong while we unconsciously create a self-fulfilling prophecy. High performers pay attention, they are aware of their surroundings, and they expect good things to happen.

Some of the best performers may get discouraged if they believe that others in the workplace are not doing their part. Many times during workshops I will ask participants, "What breaks down trust in your workplace?" One of the most common answers to this question is something similar to, "When you ask someone to do something, or expect someone else to help out, and they don't deliver." We often have high expectations of others. Star employees typically base that expectation on what they would do if they were in a similar situation.

STAR EMPLOYEES TYPICALLY BASE THAT EXPECTATION ON WHAT THEY WOULD DO IF THEY WERE IN A SIMILAR SITUATION.

Unfortunately not everyone in the workplace has the same outlook on their commitment and engagement in the organization, and more importantly, they don't have the work ethic or integrity to be proactive as they approach their work.

Keep in mind that in workplaces we need some variety. If everyone in the organization wanted to be the boss, felt that they possessed the knowledge, skills, and abilities to be the boss, and were willing to go the extra mile and fight tooth and nail for the position, we would likely have some different kinds of workplace challenge. So, your organization needs diversity in style, in personal (not organizational) vision, and expectations. It is a good thing.

Star performers need to recognize and establish that not everyone has the desire or the will to be a star. Expecting more of others may leave you very frustrated. Your boss will probably not take action and demand more performance from average performers. Expecting a little more from those with below-average performance is reasonable. Expecting those employees that perform below minimum expectations to be dealt with is absolutely reasonable.

High-performance organizations get this part correct. In fact, many of them continue to raise the bar for top performers, average performers, and those who perform just enough to get by. They do this through effective performance management systems and they realize that even the stars can be better, the average performers can continue to improve, and being sure that we are replacing the poorest non-performing employees with fully performing employees helps to raise that bar.

If you are a star, you should not love to hate those who don't live up to your standard.

GETTING ALL FIVES

It was happy hour in the fall of the year 2000. My friend Sam came scurrying into the pub with some new spring in his step. "Fours and fives!" he exclaimed. Having no idea what he was talking about I happily shouted back, "Yeah, fours and fives." He repeated, "Fours and fives. I got all fours and fives!" My curiosity increased as I asked, "What the heck are you talking about?" Sam blurted out, "I had my performance review today and I got all fours and fives!" The rest of the evening we continued to playfully repeat the joyful fours-and-fives rant.

Most workplace employees take their performance reviews very seriously. Many of the performance-review systems use a scaling approach with numbers representing one through five with a one being the worst performance and a five being the best or outstanding performance. Opinions are broad when it comes to the style, acceptance, and usefulness of job performance reviews. Many organizations use them, many do not; some think they should but they don't, and others think that they shouldn't but they do. Some bosses take them seriously; some think they are a joke.

Does your organization use performance reviews? If you are accustomed to this process and both your boss and you take this seriously, then you may be striving for all fives. Nothing can make you love to hate the boss faster than a performance review that is below your expectations.

Performance reviews should be used to help employees understand their contribution to the organization, to recognize great performance, and to help formulate future personal and career-oriented goals. Notice that I did not suggest that they should be used as a once-per-year opportunity for the boss to flex his or her muscle and blast you for the few little things you did wrong. Unfortunately, job performance reviews sometimes get a bad name because they are often used improperly.

Getting all fives is a great thing; reflecting on achievements and setting goals for the coming year is a great thing. Some bosses will never give a five, or perhaps more frequently they may give some, but rarely give fives in every category. Philosophies and strategies for performance reviews vary from organization to organization and sometimes even within the organization from boss to boss. Regardless of your organization's philosophy or that of your boss, seek to reflect on what you have accomplished and equally importantly, what you plan to do to up your game in the future.

DRAWBACKS TO BEING SIRIUS

"Pull the good out of it and not worry about the drawbacks."

~Chris Squire[3]

Life is good, the grass is always greener, and being a star performer couldn't be any keener. Make no mistake about it, being a star performer in your workplace can have its drawbacks. While many observe this position as something to aspire to, others could care less. The segment of your workplace population that could care less represents the segment to watch out for. It is this segment that can frustrate you, anger you, and sometimes make you wish you had a different job.

THE SEGMENT OF YOUR WORKPLACE POPULATION THAT COULD CARE LESS REPRESENTS THE SEGMENT TO WATCH OUT FOR.

Holding true to a love-to-hate-the-boss ideology, there are some drawbacks to being a star. Bosses have needs, and once the need is recognized, the boss will likely spring into action. Sometimes this action is to delegate some work to a fellow staff member. This is where you, the star, come in to play. You see, the boss wants it done quickly, the boss

163

wants it done accurately, and often the boss wants it done yesterday!

Here is a dirty little secret. The star performer, well, they get all the work. When the boss needs to impress, you get handed the assignment and are expected to exceed expectations. When the boss has procrastinated and is running behind schedule, you get handed the assignment. When the simplest task comes down from above and the boss is otherwise preoccupied, you get the task. I see a pattern here, do you?

Bosses are people too. I know it is hard to believe but it is true. People, especially those lacking high levels of discipline, often seek the easy road. They don't want to invite trouble, they don't want to deal with controversy, and most of all, they don't want to waste any time. Dealing with underperforming employees may invite trouble, involve controversy, and quite honestly feel (in the moment) like a waste of time. Some bosses, in a classic love-to-hate-the-boss style, give the assignment where the assignment is not only easily accepted, but is also completed to perfection. This means it has been given to you.

Sometimes we have to take the good with the bad. You have to find the balance in your work and sometimes being the star means instead of kudos, you get more work. I'm not suggesting that this should be ignored and I'm certainly not suggesting that your contribution should be taken for granted. What I am suggesting is that you make your best effort to take this all in stride and plan an appropriate moment for a discussion with your boss. Most of all, do not allow yourself to become resentful. Handling your emotions during tough times is one of the most important aspects of maintaining your self-respect and creating your future success.

CREATING YOUR LEGACY

It's hard to say what I want my legacy to be when I'm long gone.
~Aaliyah[4]

Legacy is a bold word. It may be difficult to imagine what you want your legacy to be. Unfortunately, Aaliyah's life seemed too short. She was killed when her plane crashed in 2001. She was only twenty-two years old.[5]

Life is short; we've all heard this phrase. Not everyone will care about the legacy that they leave behind in the workplace, and many will go with seemingly little impact and perhaps no legacy.

What do you want to leave behind? What do you want others to say about you when you have left your current job? A study conducted by the US Bureau of Labor and Statistics reports that the average person holds approximately eleven jobs between the ages of eighteen and forty-four.[6] Consider the number of different jobs you have encountered or what your future holds and the number you will encounter. Because life is short, your time spent in a particular job may be more limited than you realize, and unless you have a magical crystal ball you have no idea what tomorrow will bring, so now may be the time to think about your legacy.

Major metropolitan areas are different than small rural towns. The number of businesses and people that we meet will perhaps vary considerably between metro and rural. You are probably familiar with the phrase, "it's a small world," but when you are considering your career, this phrase and its associated meaning, is even more important. Word of mouth is powerful, and with social media that power is greatly expanded. Successful people think about legacy; successful people care about what others will say when they are gone.

"Don't burn your bridges," is a cliché that can often be heard echoing somewhere near the human resources office. Short, to the point, and good. Keep this in mind in your work. You never know who you will bump into in just a few short years. You never know who will become the next great business owner, senior vice president, or your boss.

Create a legacy—your legacy!

CHAPTER SUMMARY

Being a serious performer is important to many. It may be reflective of how we grow in our career. Career growth is not important to everyone and because of this we will encounter other employees who are simply not serious. I believe in the stars, I believe in big dreams, and I believe in audacious goals. I believe that with an audacious goal we will push ourselves to become more, to be better, and to be a star.

The drawbacks to being a star may include being a dumping ground for all "important" assignments. What is labeled important may be mundane and actually be a routine task that hasn't been completed due to procrastination or simple neglect.

Legacy seems like a strong word. There certainly must exist some power in your presence if you have created a legacy. It seems that legacy is not about life or about death, it is about creating a trail that says, "This is me, this is what I did and what I was about at this point in my life or career."

If you grow, your legacy will likely grow with you, likewise if you stop improving, your legacy will only be as good as your last personal best.

► As you consider your expectations of others, ask yourself the following:

1) Am I expecting too much from this person? (Even if the person in question is your boss.)

2) What can I do that would appropriately provide feedback or coaching to improve this situation?

3) Is it my responsibility to take action on this situation?

► When considering your performance review scores or evaluation think about the following:

4) Stepping back and accurately self-assessing, are the scores reasonable?

5) If I reject the performance review or argue the evaluation, what will change?

6) If I received all fives what can I do now to continue to improve my contributions and value to the organization?

► The next time you receive work that you weren't expecting or that seems beneath your capabilities, try to find the good in the process and avoid the love-to-hate scenario by asking yourself:

7) Is this an assignment where I can perform exceptionally well? If yes, then it adds to my future value.

8) What is my strategy to tactfully and appropriately discuss this with my boss?

9) Do the drawbacks to being a star outweigh the benefits?

▶   Not so sure what to think about creating your legacy? Try this:

10) What do I want to be remembered for?

11) What might others say about me if they were asked about me in private?

12) What legacy characteristics do I see in others who I view as successful? What have they done and how did they do it?

Dennis E. Gilbert

NOTES

CHAPTER 1

1. André Gide, accessed December 1, 2012, http://www.goodreads.com/quotes/list/9364382-lucky.

2. Wikipedia, accessed December 4, 2012, http://en.wikipedia.org/wiki/Harley_davidson.

3. E. L. James, accessed December 1, 2012, http://www.eljamesauthor.com/books/fifty-shades-of-grey/.

CHAPTER 2

1. "Ernest Hemingway," BrainyQuotes, accessed November 29, 2012, http://www.brainyquote.com/quotes/quotes/e/ernesthemi383060.html.

2. "Abraham Lincoln," BrainyQuotes, accessed November 29, 2012, http://www.brainyquote.com/quotes/quotes/a/abrahamlin101343.html.

3. Wikipedia, accessed November 29, 2012, http://en.wikipedia.org/wiki/Country_Strong_(soundtrack).

4. Geoffrey Fowler, "Facebook Tops Billion User Mark," *The Wall Street Journal* (October 4, 2012), http://online.wsj.com/article/SB10000872396390443 63540457803616402738612.html.

5. Wikipedia, accessed November 29, 2012, http://en.wikipedia.org/wiki/List_of_countries_by_p opulation

6. Robert B. Cialdini, "Reciprocation: The Old Give and Take...and Take," in *Influence: The Psychology of Persuasion*, 17.

7. Wikipedia, accessed November 29, 2012, http://en.wikipedia.org/wiki/Pay_It_Forward.

CHAPTER 3

1. "Margaret Thatcher," BrainyQuotes, accessed November 29, 2012, http://www.brainyquote.com/quotes/quotes/m/mar garetth138452.html.

2. Wikipedia, accessed May 1, 2012, http://en.wikipedia.org/wiki/Abilene_Paradox.

3. "Thomas Carlyle," BrainyQuotes, accessed November 29, 2012, http://www.brainyquote.com/quotes/quotes/t/thom ascarl156130.html.

4. "Norm Coleman," BrainyQuotes, accessed November 29, 2012, http://www.brainyquote.com/quotes/quotes/n/nor mcolema168786.html.

CHAPTER 4

1. "Arianna Huffington," BrainyQuotes, accessed May 16, 2012 http://www.brainyquote.com/quotes/quotes/a/arian nahuf396029.html.

2. Wikipedia, accessed April 25, 2012, http://en.wikipedia.org/wiki/Obsessive-compulsive_disorder.

3. "Obsessive-Compulsive Personality Disorder," Psych Central Staff, accessed April 25, 2012, http://psychcentral.com/disorders/sx26.htm.

4. "Franklin D. Roosevelt," BrainyQuotes, accessed November 29, 2012, http://www.brainyquote.com/quotes/quotes/f/frankl ind404172.html.

CHAPTER 5

1. "Tom Ridge," BrainyQuotes, accessed November 30, 2012, http://www.brainyquote.com/quotes/quotes/t/tomri dge195742.html.

2. "Ronald Reagan," BrainyQuotes, accessed November 30, 2012, http://www.brainyquote.com/quotes/quotes/r/ronal dreag147688.html.

3. Wikipedia, accessed November 30, 2012, http://en.wikipedia.org/wiki/Underemployment.

CHAPTER 6

1. "Zig Ziglar," BrainyQuotes, accessed November 30, 2012, http://www.brainyquote.com/quotes/quotes/z/zigzi glar381977.html.

2. "Muffin Top," Wikipedia, accessed on November 30, 2012, http://en.wikipedia.org/wiki/Muffin_top.

3. "Gene Tierney," BrainyQuotes, accessed November 30, 2012, http://www.brainyquote.com/quotes/quotes/g/genet ierne197148.html.

4. "Dr. Seuss," Goodreads, accessed on November 30, 2012, http://www.goodreads.com/author/quotes/61105.Dr _Seuss.

CHAPTER 7

1. "Mae West," BrainyQuotes, accessed November 30, 2012, http://www.brainyquote.com/quotes/quotes/m/mae west400052.html.

2. Wikipedia, accessed November 30, 2012, http://en.wikipedia.org/wiki/Appreciative_inquiry.

3. "Tony Robbins," BrainyQuotes, accessed November 30, 2012, http://www.brainyquote.com/quotes/quotes/t/tonyr obbin147791.html.

CHAPTER 8

1. "Sam Walton," BrainyQuotes, accessed December 1, 2012, http://www.brainyquote.com/quotes/quotes/s/samw alton146810.html.

2. "Stanley Milgram," BrainyQuotes, accessed May 17, 2012,
http://www.brainyquote.com/quotes/quotes/s/stanle
ymil120999.html.

CHAPTER 9

1. Archie Bunker, accessed December 2, 2012,
http://www.archiebunkerquotes.com/7.html.

2. Wikipedia, accessed December 2, 2012,
http://en.wikipedia.org/wiki/All_in_the_Family.

3. "Oreo at 100," *Chicago Tribune News*,(March 6, 2012),
http://articles.chicagotribune.com/2012-03-
06/news/ct- talk-oreos-turn-100-0306-
20120306_1_oreo-cookies-bakeries-kraft-foods.

4. "Martha Stewart," BrainyQuotes, accessed December 4, 2012,
http://www.brainyquote.com/quotes/quotes/m/mart
hast ew385891.html.

CHAPTER 10

1. "Brian Tracy," BrainyQuotes, accessed December 1, 2012, http://www.brainyquote.com/quotes/quotes/b/brian tracy452661.html.

2. "Tom Hopkins," BrainyQuotes, accessed December 1, 2012, http://www.brainyquote.com/quotes/quotes/t/tomh opkins183077.html.

3. "Chris Squire," BrainyQuotes, accessed December 1, 2012, http://www.brainyquote.com/quotes/quotes/c/chris squir202329.html.

4. "Aaliyah," BrainyQuotes, accessed December 1, 2012, http://www.brainyquote.com/quotes/quotes/a/aaliya h141206.html.

5. Wikipedia, accessed December 1, 2012, http://en.wikipedia.org/wiki/Aaliyah

6. "Number of jobs held by individuals from age 18 to age 44 in 1978 to 2008 by educational attainment, sex, race, and Hispanic or Latino ethnicity," accessed December 1, 2012, http://www.bls.gov/nls/nlsy79r23jobsbyedu.pdf.

Dennis E. Gilbert

INDEX

A

academic · 66
administrative · 77, 78, 111
advancement · 62, 104, 113, 114, 124, 128
aggressive · 119
appreciation
    appreciative · 14
appreciative inquiry · 105
argue · 21, 28, 29, 79, 97, 110, 139, 150, 168
assignment
    assignments · 44, 46, 62, 64, 77, 78, 79, 85, 164, 169
assignments · 47, 52, 53, 57, 60, 64, 67, 68, 70, 76, 78, 80, 81, 84, 112, 117, 126, 167
attitude · 47, 64, 66, 74, 93, 107, 111, 116, 117, 127
avoidance · 3, 138

B

Bosses
    boss · i, 46, 47, 48, 52, 53, 158, 163, 164
Bullies · 28

bullying
    mobbing · 2, 13
burnt out · 70
business owner
    owner · 13, 81, 146, 153, 166
Buy-in · 33

C

career path · 17, 70, 74, 107
challenge · 19, 21, 45, 74, 75, 115, 119, 147, 148, 154, 160
change · 5, 9, 14, 28, 29, 53, 54, 58, 64, 67, 73, 106, 107, 109, 113, 122, 155, 168
choices · 3, 4, 19, 28, 30, 34, 35, 37, 57, 65, 69, 70, 71, 73, 81, 89, 106, 129, 138
college. · 68, 72
committee · 106, 111, 115
comparison
    compare · 46, 56
compensation · 60, 62, 65, 66, 73, 80, 81, 82, 84, 121
conflict · 89, 99, 121, 145
consensus · 28, 35, 36, 37, 39, 41
contribution · 2, 50, 76, 118,

127, 162, 164

conversation · 49, 63, 121,
127, 135

credibility · 110, 113, 114,
125, 139

cultural shift · 118

customers
customer · 31, 33, 54, 72,
94

cyclical changes · 67

D

debate · 17, 27, 28, 32, 33

decision
decision making · 15, 28,
29, 30, 33, 35, 36, 37,
38, 39, 40, 41, 59, 73,
91, 133

Delegation · v, 43, 60

demeaning · 134

destiny · 183

direct report · 4, 24, 44, 56,
57, 58, 136

direct reports · vii, 2, 44, 48,
50, 51, 52, 53, 60, 63, 88,
96, 113, 133, 134, 137,
149, 158

disappointment · 64, 116

discouraged · 14, 24, 159

discrimination · 9, 89

disengaged · 10, 74, 75, 95

downsizing. · 49

Dress code · 88, 90, 94, 95,
99

E

earnings potential · 79

economic conditions
economic · 15, 16, 25, 67,
70, 152

effectiveness · 18, 28, 48

empowered · 56, 59, 67, 68,
70, 71

empowerment · 56, 60, 61,
80

Empowerment · v, 56, 59, 80

energy · 2, 22, 94, 100, 106,
115, 116, 119, 120

evaluation · 119, 168

experience · 183

F

family · ix, 12, 17, 66, 71, 72,
73, 74, 132, 145, 146, 147,
149, 151, 152, 153, 154,
155

fast-paced · 94

fear · ix, 4, 8, 12, 15, 31, 44,
49, 50, 51, 57, 64

feedback · 26, 52, 115, 116,
168

Firing
fire · 151

G

generation
generational · 65, 118

government · 15, 61, 113, 138
guidelines · 100, 121
guilty
guilt · 61, 117

H

harmonious
harmony · 20, 99
harmony · vii, 32, 58
hoarding · 44, 49, 57
human resource · 111, 139

I

influence · 12, 14, 18, 20, 25, 91, 127
Informal power · 13
inspired · ix, 34
investment · 25, 69

J

jealousy
jealous · 93
job description · 60, 61, 62, 84, 139, 141
job positions · 61, 66
judgment · 34, 92, 93, 111

K

knowledge · 13, 29, 30, 36,

48, 63, 72, 81, 82, 103, 104, 124, 125, 128, 139, 160

L

Leaders · 43
leadership · 13, 15, 35, 37, 59, 97, 104, 134
learning
learn · 183
legacy · 6, 165, 166, 167, 169
Listening · v, 11, 22

M

methods
method · 18, 37
micromanage · 44
mid-riff · 91
mismanaged agreement · 30, 31, 39, 40
Mismanaged agreement · 30, 31
motivation · 60, 61, 62, 64, 66, 87, 105
mundane · 74, 75, 167

N

negative fantasy · 16
networking
network · 18, 19, 25

O

obsessive-compulsive · 52
occupations · 69
Opinions · 161
opportunities · 3, 14, 28, 60,
    62, 67, 69, 75, 77, 80, 82,
    84, 85, 113, 114, 119, 121,
    123, 126, 128, 139, 159
organization · 13, 25, 26, 28,
    30, 31, 32, 41, 44, 45, 48,
    49, 51, 53, 54, 58, 59, 68,
    72, 75, 76, 78, 79, 82, 85,
    89, 95, 98, 101, 111, 117,
    118, 120, 121, 123, 124,
    128, 132, 134, 136, 138,
    139, 147, 154, 155, 157,
    158, 159, 160, 162, 168
organizational · vii, 24, 28,
    29, 30, 48, 49, 52, 54, 60,
    76, 97, 146, 147, 150, 160
over-confident · 107

P

passion · 6, 10, 51
passionate · 5, 6, 21
peer pressure · 31
Perception · 63
perceptions · 37, 63, 64, 66,
    71, 81, 127
performance · 3, 6, 15, 31,
    36, 47, 51, 52, 56, 57, 62,
    67, 78, 89, 90, 94, 96, 100,
    106, 111, 112, 114, 115,
    116, 119, 120, 121, 123,
    127, 128, 140, 148, 154,
    156, 157, 158, 160, 161,
    162, 168, 183
perks · 62
persuasion · 14, 20, 36, 37
political power play · 133,
    135, 141
population · 158, 163
Power · 12, 13, 24, 132
pressure · 14, 54
prioritization · 48
privately held · 135
productivity · 10, 93, 97, 137
provocative · 93
psychology · 8, 52, 108

Q

qualifications · 107, 108, 109,
    125

R

rate of pay · 65, 69
reciprocity · 12, 19, 24, 25,
    26
responsibility · 3, 4, 51, 54,
    66, 67, 72, 73, 80, 99, 109,
    124, 135, 168
rightsizing · 67
risk · ix, 21, 26, 27, 50, 56,
    109, 115, 120, 121, 138
Rules · 7, 95

S

self-assessment · 22, 63, 75, 108
self-promotion · 113
social media · 17, 18, 166
stakeholders · 31, 33, 72
star · 8, 35, 47, 116, 157, 158, 160, 161, 163, 164, 167, 169
status quo · 51, 54
strategy · 21, 32, 76, 169
success · ix, 2, 3, 4, 10, 12, 14, 23, 27, 32, 33, 43, 50, 51, 52, 67, 68, 87, 90, 101, 105, 109, 115, 118, 120, 135, 136, 143, 149, 154, 165
Successful · 4, 32, 60, 166
surveys · 31
survival · vii, 35, 36, 134

T

Talent · 103, 124
team · 22, 29, 30, 31, 33, 35, 39, 44, 56, 59, 70, 81, 83, 97, 115, 116, 118, 126, 134, 140
technology · 15, 29, 113, 119, 138
training · 183
trust · 62, 70, 124, 126, 134, 136, 159

U

unconsciously · 34, 138, 159
underemployed · 70, 73, 74, 84

V

visible
  visibility · 112, 113, 114, 115, 121, 122, 126, 157
volunteer · 112, 126

W

wage · 64, 124
well balanced · 107

Dennis E. Gilbert

ABOUT THE AUTHOR

Mr. Dennis E. Gilbert is the president of Appreciative Strategies, LLC, a human performance improvement training and consulting business. He combines his expertise in private for-profit business management with his experience in the non-profit educational sector to deliver outstanding results through consultation and training interventions. His extensive background in management and education is the culmination of over twenty-five years of experience with both for-profit businesses and non-profit institutions of higher learning.

Dennis published the popular book: *90/90, Ninety Inspirational Messages, Ninety Seconds to Success* in May 2012.

Dennis helps people and organizations discover their destiny. He is a consultant, trainer, speaker, and author who is available for worldwide engagements.

For more information visit his website:

http://DennisEGilbert.com